A LIVING GOSPEL

Also by Robert Ellsberg

All Saints: Daily Reflections on Saints, Prophets, and Witnesses for Our Time

Blessed Among All Women: Reflections on Women Saints, Prophets, and Witnesses for Our Time

Blessed Among Us: Day by Day with Saintly Witnesses

The Franciscan Saints

Hearts on Fire: The Story of the Maryknoll Sisters (with Penny Lernoux and Arthur Jones)

The Saints' Guide to Happiness

As editor:

All the Way to Heaven: Selected Letters of Dorothy Day

Carlo Carretto: Essential Writings

Charles de Foucauld: Selected Writings

Dorothy Day: Selected Writings

The Duty of Delight: The Diaries of Dorothy Day

Flannery O'Connor: Spiritual Writings

Fritz Eichenberg: Works of Mercy

Gandhi on Christianity

A Harvey Cox Reader

Modern Spiritual Masters: Writings on Contemplation and Compassion

A Penny a Copy: Readings from The Catholic Worker (with Jim Forest and Tom Cornell)

Pope Francis, *The Courage to be Happy: The Pope Speaks to the Youth of the World*

Pope Francis, *A Stranger and You Welcomed Me: A Call to Solidarity with Migrants and Refugees*

Thich Nhat Hanh: Essential Writings

A LIVING GOSPEL

Reading God's Story in Holy Lives

Robert Ellsberg

ORBIS BOOKS
Maryknoll, New York 10545

Founded in 1970, Orbis Books endeavors to publish works that enlighten the mind, nourish the spirit, and challenge the conscience. The publishing arm of the Maryknoll Fathers and Brothers, Orbis seeks to explore the global dimensions of the Christian faith and mission, to invite dialogue with diverse cultures and religious traditions, and to serve the cause of reconciliation and peace. The books published reflect the views of their authors and do not represent the official position of the Maryknoll Society. To learn more about Maryknoll and Orbis Books, please visit our website at www.maryknollsociety.org.

Copyright © 2019 by Robert Ellsberg

Published by Orbis Books, Box 302, Maryknoll, NY 10545-0302.

PHOTO CREDITS: p. 12, © Office Central de Lisieux; pp., 26, 29, 34, 37, 42, 47, courtesy Marquette University archives; p. 51 © Bob Fitch; p. 59 photo of Thomas Merton, used with permission of the Merton Legacy Trust and the Thomas Merton Center at Bellarmine University; p. 71, photo by Thomas Merton, used with permission of the Merton Legacy Trust and the Thomas Merton Center at Bellarmine University; p. 63, © Jim Forest; pp. 76, 79, 80, 87 courtesy, Henri Nouwen Literary Center; p. 85 © Peter Weiskel; p. 91, courtesy Ina Dillar Russell Library, Georgia College & State University; pp. 143, 155 courtesy Maryknoll Mission Archives; p. 160, by Monica Olson.

Manufactured in the United States of America

Library of Congress Cataloging-in-Publication Data

Names: Ellsberg, Robert, 1955- author.
Title: A living Gospel : reading God's story in holy lives / Robert Ellsberg.
Description: Maryknoll : Orbis Books, 2019. | Includes bibliographical
   references and index.
Identifiers: LCCN 2018057638 (print) | LCCN 2019007232 (ebook) | ISBN
   9781608337866 (ebook) | ISBN 9781626983250 (pbk.)
Subjects: LCSH: Christian biography. | Christian life.
Classification: LCC BR1690 (ebook) | LCC BR1690 .E45 2019 (print) | DDC
   282.092/2 [B]—dc23
LC record available at https://lccn.loc.gov/2018057638

To Monica and Sister Wendy

"It is true that those we meet can change us,
sometimes so profoundly that we are not the same afterwards,
even unto our names."

—Yann Martel, *Life of Pi*

CONTENTS

INTRODUCTION
The Making of a Saint-Watcher

> *The Holy Spirit writes no more gospels except in our hearts. All we do from moment to moment is live this new gospel of the Holy Spirit. We, if we are holy, are the paper; our sufferings and our actions are the ink. The workings of the Holy Spirit are his pen, and with it he writes a living gospel.*
> —Jean-Pierre de Caussade, SJ (1675–1751)

FOUR STOUT VOLUMES of *Butler's Lives of the Saints* dominate the shelf above my desk. They were a gift I made to myself, though it was a significant investment, some months after becoming a

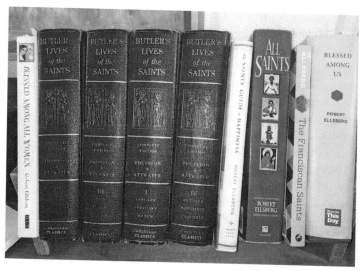

Catholic in 1980. A friend had given me a much smaller dictionary of saints with the inscription, "Welcome to the Catholic Church. The saints are the best thing about us." After spending five years working with Dorothy Day at the Catholic Worker community in New York City, I had no doubt that this was true. If there was anything that particularly attracted me to Catholicism it was less the persuasive power of doctrine or theology, which I comprehended only dimly, than the example of holy men and women—both those I had read about and those I had met.

In the years that followed I would read and annotate every page of those four volumes, as well as the twelve volumes of a later modern edition. There has not been a day when their stories—some inspiring, some incomprehensibly strange, and others like windows into heaven—haven't come to mind.

And over time I woke to a surprising fact: that I had somehow become a *hagiographer*. That fancy word describes someone who writes about saints or holy people. It is a word that has fallen into disrepute. Hagiography has become identified with a particularly saccharine, credulous, and pious style of writing that conforms its subjects to a stereotypical mold—the proverbial "plaster saint."

Thomas Merton described this figure as a person "without the slightest moral flaw...[whose] intentions are the noblest...[whose] words are always the most edifying clichés, fitting the situation with a devastating obviousness that silences even the thought of dialogue." Such saints, he wrote, are presumed to be "without humor, as they are without wonder, without feeling, and without interest in the common affairs of mankind...They are always there kissing the leper's sores at the very moment when the king and his noble attendants come around the corner and stop in their tracks, mute in admiration."[1]

If that's what it means to be a saint—close to God, but somehow less than fully human—then (to borrow a phrase from Flannery O'Connor) to hell with it.[2] But Merton goes on to observe that holiness is really a matter of being more fully human: "This implies a greater capacity for concern, for suffering, for understanding, for sympathy, and also for humor, for joy, for appreciation for the good and beautiful things of life."[3]

This suggests that it is not so much the word "hagiography" that is in need of rehabilitation as the concept of holiness itself. Too often, as Dorothy Day observes, the lives of the saints are written "as though they were not in this world." She continues, "We have seldom been given the saints as they really were..."[4] In striving to write about such men and women as they truly were, I hope to show how much we can learn from them—not just about what it means to be a Christian but about what it means to be a fully realized human being. After all, as Day writes, "The saint is the holy person, the 'whole' person, the integrated person." She adds, "We all wish to be that..."[5]

My own contributions began with a book called *All Saints: Daily Reflections on Saints, Prophets, and Witnesses for Our Time.*[6] The title was inspired by the feast of All Saints on November 1, a day set aside to remember not only the officially recognized or canonized saints but also the vast number of holy men and women known only to God. It was a book shaped first of all by my experience at the Catholic Worker. Thus, along with entries on traditional saints (Augustine, Francis of Assisi, Teresa of Avila), I included many figures beyond the official canon, including writers, artists, peacemakers, and modern martyrs—365 in all, one for each day of the year. (It is a sign of my prescience—or, more likely, the wisdom of the church—that in the past twenty years a full forty of "my" saints, including Pope John XXIII, Mother Teresa, Oscar Romero, Sr. Thea Bowman, and Dorothy Day herself, have been added to the official canon, or have had their causes set in motion.)

My aim was first of all to take the saints down from their pedestals—to show them as actual human beings who lived in a particular historical moment and who tried as best they could to follow where God was leading them. But I also had another purpose. Simone Weil wrote that today it is not nearly enough merely to be a saint, "but we must have the saintliness demanded by the present moment."[7] What is the saintliness demanded by *our* moment? Working backwards from that question, I let my intuition guide me to figures from far and wide and across the centuries: from Noah and the prophet Amos to Pierre Teilhard de Chardin and the novelist Flannery O'Connor. I hoped, at the same time, to enlarge the popular understanding of holiness beyond the restrictive Catholic boundaries. Thus, I included figures like Gandhi, Anne Frank, Vincent van Gogh, and Rabbi Abraham Heschel, who wrote: "Holiness is not the monopoly of any particular religion or tradition. Wherever a deed is done in accord with the will of God, wherever a human thought is directed toward Him, there is the holy."[8]

I presumed that my first book on the subject would also be my last, but others followed: *Blessed Among All Women*, on women saints; *The Saints' Guide to Happiness*; *Modern Spiritual Masters*; and, recently, *The Franciscan Saints*. In 2010 Liturgical Press invited me to write a daily reflection on saints and holy people for *Give Us This Day*, a monthly resource for prayer. What began as a two-year commitment has continued to the present day, nine years later.

A selection of those pieces, two per day, was eventually collected in *Blessed Among Us*.[9] It contains entries on well-known saints, along with others who are fairly obscure, including those canonized in recent decades. But there are also many men and women beyond the list of actual or prospective Catholic saints. Most readers of *Give Us This Day* have apparently understood and appreciated this eclectic sensibility. Others have been put off, resulting in canceled subscriptions and the occasional letter of protest.

It was surely Dorothy Day who inspired me in this approach. To Dorothy the saints were not just heavenly patrons but friends and companions. Their images illustrated the pages of her newspaper; their names popped up in daily conversation: St. Joseph, patron of the Catholic Worker, who was himself a worker and provider for his holy family; St. Benedict, father of Western monasticism, who promoted the life of community as a path to holiness and who lauded manual labor as a form of prayer; St. Teresa of Avila, who would raise the spirits of her sisters by dancing on the table with castanets; or Dorothy's favorite, St. Therese of Lisieux, the Carmelite nun whose teaching on the "Little Way" probably shaped Dorothy's spirituality more than any other. And then there was St. Francis, who set out to reform the church by imitating the radical poverty of the Poor Man Jesus.

But you needn't have spent much time with Dorothy Day to know that she drew inspiration from a much wider cloud of witnesses, including Gandhi, Tolstoy, martyrs of the labor struggle, peacemakers and prophets like Cesar Chavez and Dom Helder Camara, and even fictional characters in the novels of Dostoevsky or Ignacio Silone. Her writing and conversation were filled with such figures, and over time they would become my guides and companions as well.

It is a mistake to think that only officially canonized saints can open our hearts to the sacred, or inspire us to love our neighbors or stand up for a just cause. The power of great minds and souls is not restricted to those who pass the rigorous test of canonization. I find encouragement from no less a source than Pope Francis, who organized his talk before Congress in 2015 around "four great Americans": Abraham Lincoln, Martin Luther King Jr., Thomas Merton, and Dorothy Day herself—only two of them Catholics, only one of them an actual candidate for canonization. Such figures, he said, offer "a new way of seeing and interpreting reality." In those words, I dare say the pope has also offered a new way of seeing and interpreting the function of saints.

But that wide perspective extends far beyond Pope Francis or Dorothy Day. We might trace it back to the gospels and see how often Jesus looked past the good religious people of his day to exalt those on the margins—whether outsiders, foreigners, or "sinners"—as models of faith or charity. We should also recall how Jesus described the criteria of our salvation: "I was hungry and you fed me . . . I was a stranger and you welcomed me . . ."

That verse supplied the foundation of the Catholic Worker and the work of so many other saints. I have included them in my books. But there are others—some obscure, perhaps not Christian, not entirely orthodox, not entirely pure, whom I am confident God will welcome into paradise before those of us who fail the test of mercy. I do not hold them up as candidates for canonization, but in the hope that through their stories we might hear the voice that calls us further, deeper.

And so now I have written another book, drawing on many years of reflection on holy lives and what they have to teach us.

These lessons are embodied not only in figures encountered in the pages of *Butler's Lives,* but in the lives of men and women of our own time, some of whom I was privileged to know. Among other things, they teach us that the path of holiness is not straightforward; it is not marked by a tally of achievements or mystical insights to be checked off a list. It is a lifelong journey in which we strive, mostly by small steps, to grow in faith, hope, and love. Like every journey, it is marked by twists and turns, advances and setbacks. In the case of a Christian, this is the process by which the pattern of Christ's life, death, and resurrection becomes the pattern of our own lives; the logic of Christ's message becomes the logic by which we live. As the great Alban Butler put it in the introduction to his *Lives,* the saints are "the gospel, clothed, as it were, in a body."

Still, to speak of people who pursue this path as "saints" may lead us astray, since we tend to identify the word "saint" only with those exceptional figures who have been officially canonized. In his letters to the communities in Corinth and in other places St. Paul referred to all the Christians he addressed—not just the spiritual prodigies among them—as "the saints." This was not because they were likely to be canonized (a process that wouldn't exist for another thousand years). Rather, it was an indication that all Christians could be characterized or identified by their goal, the object of their striving; they were saints by virtue of their calling and desire to be saints.

Like us, the saints were people of flesh and blood, struggling to find their way, not knowing exactly where their path would take them. In this book I have focused less on their teachings or spiritual wisdom than on what Jean-Pierre de Caussade, a French Jesuit from the eighteenth century, called the "living gospel" that is written in their lives.[10] The emphasis is not so much on the things they said or did, but on how, as Pope Francis has put it, they encountered God "along the path." And so, in this book, I have included chapters on several figures who have served as companions and guides on my own path: Dorothy Day, Thomas Merton, Henri Nouwen, Charles de Foucauld, and Flannery O'Connor. They are not canonized saints (though Foucauld has been beatified and

Day's cause is in process); they all had their limitations. Yet they serve my primary purpose: to reflect on the story of God that is written in holy lives. My hope is that, through reflection on such witnesses, we may learn to read our own story with new eyes.

So many of the saints themselves began their journeys through an encounter with another saint—whether in person, or more often through reading. I think of St. Augustine, still wavering over his own conversion, who came across the *Life of St. Antony*, an early Desert Father, and was "astonished to hear of the wonders [God] had worked so recently, almost in our own times."[11] Or Edith Stein (St. Teresa Benedicta of the Cross), a German philosopher raised in an Orthodox Jewish home, at the time an agnostic, who stayed up all night reading the *Autobiography* of St. Teresa of Avila, and, as the sun rose, put down the book and said, "This is the truth." It was an important step that led to her conversion, her entry into a Carmelite monastery, and ultimately her death in the gas chamber at Auschwitz. René Voillaume and Madeleine Hutin independently read an early biography of Blessed Charles de Foucauld, the modern-day Desert Father, and, like Augustine, astonished by the wonders God was working in their own time, were inspired to found congregations based on his effort to emulate the "hidden life" of Jesus in Nazareth.

Call me a hagiographer, if you like—or perhaps a "saint-watcher," or just a chronicler of lives well lived: this work has

become my own spiritual path. It is a sacred calling, insofar as it holds the possibility that some person, somewhere, might read about one of these lives and respond, as did St. Ignatius of Loyola after reading about the saints, by wondering, "What if I should live like that?"

At the end of the day, as I must constantly remember, the important thing is not to be a hagiographer, but *to be a saint*. Ultimately, that is my own struggle, as it is yours. How do we do this? Where shall we do this? As Thomas Merton wrote, "Somewhere, nowhere, beyond all 'where.'"[12]

There is no better time or place than the present.

THE CALL TO HOLINESS

MY LOCAL PARISH CHURCH, like many others, is adorned with stained glass windows that depict a range of famous and, in some cases, not-so-famous, saints. No doubt the conception that many Catholics have of saints is largely inspired by such images. There may have been a time when every child in the parish school could recount the stories represented in those windows. They would know that *St. Agnes* was a virgin martyr, that *St. Brendan* sailed all over the North Sea in a tiny raft, and that *St. Patrick* drove the serpents out of Ireland. Few perhaps would have known that *St. Winifred* was a Welsh maiden who was beheaded by an amorous suitor after she had resisted his advances (though they
would surely have enjoyed the
legend that her head was mirac-
ulously restored to her body by
her saintly uncle).

I doubt that today even
many adult members of the
parish would recognize all these
figures—or some who are even
more obscure: *St. Philomena, St.
Paschal,* or *St. Peter of Alcan-
tara*, a Spanish saint who slept
only one and a half hours a night
for forty years and who is depicted clutching the whip with
which he regularly disciplined
himself.

What are people supposed to learn from such images? That saints were men and women from an antique past who performed extraordinary acts of self-denial, who were capable of miraculous feats, and who died in terrible ways? That they were generally nuns and priests and bishops who spent their lives in prayer, or, as Pope Francis says, "swooning in mystic rapture," but who had little knowledge of, and perhaps even less interest in, the lives of ordinary believers?

The French novelist Léon Bloy once said that there is only one sadness: not to be a saint. Judging from the expressions on the faces of these images, we might be more inclined to suspect the opposite: that there could be no sadder fate than to end up like one of these figures in a stained glass window, clutching the instruments of our mortification.

SINCE THE EARLIEST DAYS of Christianity the church has encouraged the memory of exemplary Christians—those who offered a heroic witness to the gospel by their manner of living, their example of faith, service, and intimacy with Christ —even, in many cases, to the laying down of their lives. The Roman Empire offered many opportunities to display that kind of faith.

St. Polycarp

Those who died in the arena were a reminder of Christ's prediction that his followers should be prepared to meet his own fate. Their lives were a kind of reenactment of Christ's passion and a powerful witness to their faith in his promise of eternal life. So it was said of St. Polycarp, a bishop who died as a martyr in the second century, that his was a death "conformable to the gospel." Thus, the martyrs were a kind of living link to Jesus—a sign of God's ongoing presence among the people of God.

The early Christians venerated the memory of these witnesses; they preserved their remains and gathered at their graves on the anniversaries of their deaths. This was the origin of the cult of saints. Nevertheless, as the era of persecution faded, it became clear that there were other ways—no less heroic—of living out one's faith in the world. New models of holiness emerged: desert monastics, teachers, missionaries, servants of the poor. They too were remembered as saints. They walked the path of discipleship and reminded Christians of what it means to be a true follower of Christ.

But gradually a shift occurred in the popular relationship to saints. Rather than seeing them as a source of inspiration, Christians started to look on such figures as a locus of divine energy. Miracles were attributed to their relics. The stories of their lives became increasingly embellished by accounts of supernatural powers. In the popular imagination, saints took on the features of wonderworkers, heavenly patrons who had God's ear and could do us favors.

Over time (in part to check over-credulous local enthusiasm), the Vatican assumed authority over naming saints—the often-prolonged and bureaucratic process of canonization. This now has four stages, each marked by a particular title: *Servant of God*, after the Vatican has authorized the beginning of a "cause" for canonization; *Venerable*, once all testimony has been collected and the saint's orthodoxy has been assured; *Blessed,* after a miracle has been certified (waived in the case a martyr); and *Saint*, the final stage of canonization, following the authorization of a second miracle. During the course of many centuries, thousands of names were added to the official list—in fact, a thousand of them just in the time of Pope John Paul II, who was a regular dynamo when it came to naming saints. The balance of saints, in modern times, was shifted back from wonderworkers to exemplary witnesses of faith and charity.

Pope Francis has continued this tradition, if at a slower pace. Among the notable saints he has canonized are three recent popes, John XXIII, Paul VI, and John Paul II, as well as Mother Teresa of Calcutta and Oscar Romero. But apart from the naming of official saints, Pope Francis has tried to put the emphasis on a particular point: that all Christians are called to holiness, something much broader and more general than simply meeting the restrictive criteria for canonization.

If this idea is unfamiliar or seems implausible, it may be the process of canonization itself that is largely to blame. The singling out of certain exceptional Christians for veneration can foster the impression that a saint is altogether different from the rest of us—a kind of "perfect" person, worthy of admiration, but no more capable of inspiring our imitation than an Olympic athlete or a musical prodigy. ("I'm no Mother Teresa," one often hears—signifying a standard of charity so far beyond the capacities of "normal" people that there is no point in trying.) Their luminous reputation for miracles, their feats of asceticism or heroic martyrdom further set these saints apart from ordinary Christians.

Happily, we are called not to be prodigies or geniuses of the spiritual life but to be followers of Christ. The original disciples were not extraordinary human specimens. In Jesus they saw something that attracted them, and when they asked, "Where are you staying?" and he answered "Come and see," they decided to tag along. They watched and observed how he lived. And they continued to follow, even after his death and resurrection.

That all Christians are called to holiness is not just a notion of Pope Francis. It is the title of a section of *Lumen Gentium,* the Vatican II document on the church, which Francis cites: "Strengthened by so many and such great means of salvation, all the faithful, whatever their condition or state, are called by the Lord—each in his or her own way—to that perfect holiness by which the Father himself is perfect" (*LG* 11).

In 2018 Pope Francis issued his own apostolic exhortation on "the call to holiness in today's world" (*Gaudate et Exsultate,* or "Rejoice and Be Glad").[1] Picking up on that passage from Vatican II, he underscores the phrase, *"each in his or her own way."*

The call to holiness is not a matter of conforming ourselves to some cookie-cutter pattern or imitating certain heroic examples. Regardless of whether we are priests, nuns, or laypeople, regardless of whether we are celibate or married, have exceptional abilities or are completely average, there is a path to holiness that takes account of our particular gifts and duties in life, a path that is different for each one of us. And all Christians are called to walk that path, whose

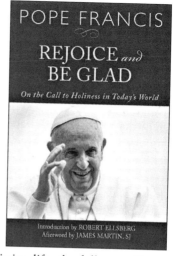

goal is simply the fullness of Christian life, the fullness of love. For this we were created—as Francis says, "not to settle for a bland and mediocre existence" (*GE* 1).

We are of course inspired and assisted by the example and encouragement of those who have advanced before us on this path—the "great cloud of witnesses" who surround us. But, as Francis makes clear, these witnesses are not just the great official saints. They may include "our mothers, grandmothers, or other loved ones. Their lives may not always have been perfect, yet even amid their faults and failings they kept moving forward and proved pleasing to the Lord" (*GE* 3).

Pope Francis speaks of those who represent "the middle class of holiness"—those whose acts of love and fidelity may earn little notice in history. He reflects on the holiness present in our "next-door neighbors," and in "the patience of God's people: in those parents who raise their children with immense love, in those men and women who work hard to support their families, in the sick, in elderly religious who never lose their smile" (*GE* 7). We are all, he says, "called to be holy by living our lives with love and by bearing witness in everything we do, wherever we find ourselves" (*GE* 14). He associates sanctity with *patience*—not just in the usual sense but "also as a constancy in going forward, day by day." This, he says, "was the sanctity of my parents: my dad, my mom, my grandmother, Rosa, who loved me so much."[2]

Sanctity may be all around us; nevertheless, the ranks of canonized saints—even in recent years—remain overwhelmingly populated by priests, bishops, and members of religious orders. Traditionally, that reflected the bias of a two-tiered spiritual hierarchy that set religious life apart from the secular world, and thus, supposedly, closer to heaven. In more recent times it more likely reflects the fact that religious orders have the time and resources to invest in the lengthy process of saint-making—hence, the preponderance of holy founders, of which there seems to be an inexhaustible supply. In contrast, apart from martyrs, the church has traditionally found it difficult to recognize the features of lay holiness, whether expressed in professional life, in common labor, or in the context of the family. With the canonization of Louis and Zelie Martin in 2015, the church recognized for the first time a couple whose holiness was expressed in married life. But, even in this case, their reputation for holiness doubtless rested on the fame of their daughter, St. Therese of Lisieux, a cloistered nun. In memorializing her parents, St. Therese elevated the status of lay sanctity. But that was not the only way that this Carmelite nun called attention to the holiness of ordinary life.

Therese Martin was born in Normandy in 1873. Following the death of her mother, when Therese was four, she and her four older sisters were left in the care of their father, a pious watchmaker. When she was fifteen Therese received a special dispensation (in light of her young age) to enter the Carmelite convent of Lisieux, where two of her sisters had already preceded her. The rest of her short life was spent within the cloister of this obscure convent. She died of tuberculosis on September 30, 1897 at the age of twenty-four.[3]

Early in life, Therese had determined that she wished to be a saint, and even as a child she had devised a method. She called it "the Little Way." It was an effort to respond with love to each chore, encounter, or petty insult that made up her daily life. She believed that by the practice of this discipline she could take the

St. Therese of Lisieux

ordinary business of life and convert it into the fuel of sanctity. Every situation might become an arena for holiness. And by the small, molecular influence of each action and intention, she might transform the world.

In her case, the road to holiness included all the daily "pinpricks of community life": the sister with an annoying habit of fidgeting with her rosary or the one who inadvertently splashed dirty water on her while doing the laundry. Each of these was an occasion to restrain the impulse to judgment and resentment, to enlarge her capacity for patience and forgiveness.

Ultimately Therese's sufferings amounted to considerably more than the "pinpricks" of community life. After contracting a virulent form of tuberculosis, she spent her final months in agony of body and spirit. Toward the end, she said, she faced every form of temptation, including the specter of despair. But she held fast to her method, convinced that in this faithfulness lay the arena for her witness and the guarantee of her eventual victory.

Such a short and outwardly uneventful life might have made little impression on the world had it not been for the autobiography that Therese wrote under obedience. Published after her death, *The Story of a Soul* immediately struck a responsive chord. Her name quickly circled the globe, and Therese was declared a saint in 1925. On the centenary of her death in 1997 Pope John Paul II declared her a Doctor of the Church.

Though her emphasis on "littleness" and meekness could be interpreted in line with traditional roles assigned to women, Therese possessed a will of steel and the heart of a warrior. Identifying with her favorite saint, Joan of Arc, she demonstrated the potential power that resides in what is typically dismissed as insignificant or unimportant. Therese showed that everyday life—

the chores and encounters that make up most lives, could supply the opportunity to exercise real heroism—and that even a life of obscurity could open a path toward spiritual greatness. In Therese's autobiography she confessed a calling to every vocation, to be a warrior, a priest, a Doctor of the Church, and a martyr. In the end she came to realize that her vocation was nothing less than Charity itself, a virtue embracing every other vocation. "My vocation is love!...In the heart of the Church, who is my Mother, *I will be love.* So I shall be everything and so my dreams will be fulfilled."

Therese's spirituality, though expressed in the context of a Carmelite convent, in fact points to a model of faithfulness lived out in the exercise of ordinary life in the world. To speak of *being love* may sound sentimental and vague. But for Therese it was practical and concrete. It wasn't just a matter of feelings or passive suffering. It could mean offering a smile, regardless of your mood; paying attention to a lonely soul who is naturally boring; or, as St. John of the Cross put it, putting love where there is no love. (Doing this, he assured us, we are bound to "draw love out.") There may be few who are called to do great things, to witness before princes, or to shoulder the cross of martyrdom. Yet, as Therese demonstrated, there is a principle of continuity between our response to the everyday situations in which we find ourselves and the "great" arenas in which the saints and martyrs offered their witness.

Among those who took this message to heart was Dorothy Day, the founder of the Catholic Worker movement, whose very public life would seem to share little in common with Therese's life in the cloister. And yet Day would come to see in Therese not only a great saint but one with a message particularly relevant to our times.

Her devotion to St. Therese is all the more striking in light of her initial reaction. Upon first reading Therese's autobiography, which she received from a priest soon after her conversion, Day found it "colorless, monotonous, too small in fact for my notice." In short: "pious pap." "What kind of a saint was this who felt that she had to practice heroic charity in eating what was put in front of her, in taking medicine, enduring cold and heat, restraint, enduring the society of mediocre souls, in follow-ing the strict regime of the convent of Carmelite nuns which she had joined at the age of fifteen?"[4]

What accounted for Day's change of heart? The answer lay in her experience with the Catholic Worker. Through years of liv-ing among the poor and unwanted, enduring not only cold and heat but also the sights and smells of squalor, she came to appre-ciate the power of Therese's Little Way. Many charged that her own practice of the Works of Mercy offered no real answer to the problems of modern society. Many felt that her pacifism and small protests against nuclear war were naïve, foolish, and irrel-evant. It was in this light that Dorothy Day came to appreciate Therese's message. From Therese Dorothy learned that each sac-rifice endured in love, each work of mercy, might increase the balance of love in the world. And she extended this principle to the social sphere.

Day spent many years writing a book about Therese because, she said, she wanted to call attention to the "social implications" of her teachings: the significance of all the little things we do—or fail to do. This includes the protests we make. Appearing fool-ish while standing on a street corner with a sign for peace, or handing out a leaflet, or going to jail for a few days: each one of these gestures, though apparently foolish and ineffective, no more than a pebble in a pond, might send forth ripples that could trans-form the world.

In the gospels this principle was illustrated in the story of Jesus' multiplication of the loaves and fishes. Dorothy drew on that image for the title of one of her books. There she wrote, "One of the greatest evils of the day among those outside the proximity of the suffering poor is their sense of futility. Young people say, 'What good can one person do? What is the sense of our small effort?' They cannot see that we must lay one brick at a time, take one step at a time; we can be responsible only for the action of the present moment, but we can beg for an increase of love in our hearts that will vitalize and transform all our indi-vidual actions, and know that God will take them and multiply them, as Jesus multiplied the loaves and fishes."[5]

MANY OTHERS, in different ways, have taken up this challenge to seek the way of holiness in everyday life. Another example is Madeleine Delbrêl, the daughter of a railroad worker, who was born in France in 1904. She had spent her youth as a confirmed atheist, but when, at the age of twenty-four, she became convinced of God's existence, she saw no alternative but to dedicate herself to God's service. She considered becoming a nun but ultimately discerned that her vocation was in the world. God might call some people to stand apart, she decided, but "there are those he leaves among the crowds...These are the people who have an ordinary job, an ordinary household, or an ordinary celibacy. People with ordinary sicknesses, and ordinary times of grieving ... These are the people of ordinary life, the people we might meet on any street." Casting her lot with this anonymous crowd, she declared, "We, the ordinary people of the street, believe with all our might that this street, this world, where God has placed us, is our place of holiness."[6]

With several friends she conceived the idea of a small lay community dedicated to leading a contemplative Christian life in the midst of the world. They prepared themselves for three years, praying, studying scripture, and taking courses in social work. Then in 1933 they set forth for Ivry, a working-class city near Paris and a stronghold of the French Communist Party.

Madeleine Delbrêl

From the start, the local pastor had trouble comprehending what they were up to. Having expected that they would occupy themselves with parish duties, he was perplexed when they seemed more interested in spending time with their comemunist neighbors. They called themselves "missionaries without a boat"—not traveling overseas, but crossing the borders of faith to bear witness to the gospel in friendship and solidarity.

When asked how she prayed, Delbrêl described her "prayer of the agenda." It was simply a heightened awareness of the presence of God in all the ordinary activities of life—whether meeting people, answering the phone, or running errands. In these ordinary circumstances, she insisted, a person could experience the deepest spiritual dimensions of life.

> Each tiny act is an extraordinary event, in which heaven is given to us, in which we are able to give heaven to others. It makes no difference what we do . . . Whatever it is, it's just the outer shell of an amazing inner reality: the soul's encounter, renewed at each moment, in which the soul grows in grace and becomes ever more beautiful for her God. Is the doorbell ringing? Quick, open the door! It's God coming to love us . . . Is it time to sit down for lunch? Let's go—it's God coming to love us. Let's let him.[7]

The apostolic life of Madeleine Delbrêl or Dorothy Day, even if unconventional in the annals of the saints, may still seem far removed from the experience of "ordinary" people. But the basic principle applies to any situation. As St. Therese noted, "Holiness consists simply in doing God's will, and being just what God wants us to be."

WHILE WORKING ON MY BOOK on women saints, I was moved by the death of a dear friend and my son's godmother, Daria Donnelly. Daria was born in Pittsburgh to a large, loving, and devoutly Catholic family. She received a doctorate in English literature. Later, while working as an editor of *Commonweal*, she engaged in many quiet ministries. Soon after the birth of her second child she discovered that she had a rare and deadly form of cancer, multiple myeloma, that caused her bones to break. Like anyone under such circumstances, she felt the terrible injustice of this news. But she proved to be unusually prepared—both by faith and discipline—to face her ordeal. She accommodated herself to her circumstances with a calm, unselfish, and benevolent balance that more than ever became the mark of her personality. She was determined to make each remaining day a witness to life, and to make this her legacy to her children and those she loved.

She endured the devastating rigors of two stem-cell replacements —the sickness, the weakness, the vulnerability to every germ and jolt. She took it all in, both the bitterness and the sweetness of life. "My getting sick," she wrote, "has increased my attention to the everyday heroism of refugees, the depressed, the arthritic, the mourning, the lonely, all those who know how good it is simply to get through a day."

She remained intimately connected to the life of her church in Boston, even as it was rocked by scandal. As often as she could she received communion from a eucharistic minister. Yet there was nothing sentimental or parochial about her faith; it was simply the ground she walked on, the air she breathed. As her pastor noted, "She was to her core a woman of symbol, of story, of sacrament. She reached in the deepest Catholic sense toward the loving, nourishing, reconciling grace of God through the ordinary, commonplace things of God's created universe."

She appreciated and encouraged my writing about women saints, but she urged me to include examples of ordinary women, especially mothers, and those who knew the spiritual challenge of finding God amid the chaos and distractions of family life. Of my previous book of saints she had written me in her characteristically zany email style: "Your book was full of insight and sharp people but where are the kids? That's not your fault: does our church ever give the high five to saintly parents??? The noise the joy the distraction: Nouwen, Merton, the modern prophets, they don't have kids, and as a result they can't sort all the noise of culture, and their diagnosis is limited. Saints use it all. Anyway, it depresses me that there seems to be so little recognition of the saint mother saint father. I'm overtuned to the kids I am sure, but since

Daria Donnelly

the sickle man came calling here I am like thy will be done, hell no I won't go, kids need their mothers."

Though her initial prognosis was a matter of months, she lived on for nearly three years, grateful for each extra day to be with her husband, to watch their children grow, to add to their store of memories and their reservoir of love. She died in 2004 at the age of forty-five, as I was completing my book; I knew at once that I should include her story. In fact, I would receive more comment on her story than about any other essay in the book. She exemplified as much as any of the "great saints" the real vocation each of us faces—to embrace God's love and to reflect it back toward the world. It was reflected in her capacity to feel joy, sorrow, outrage, and hope in all the appropriate ways.

Before she died she wrote to my young daughter, commending her role in rescuing an aged horse: "The only thing that matters is showing love and compassion in the time that is given us. Your love for Leroy has altered the universe."

WHETHER IN ST. THERESE OR DOROTHY DAY, Madeleine Delbrêl or Daria Donnelly, we find a holistic spirituality, impatient with abstraction, well prepared to recognize and embrace the sacred depths of everyday experience, whether of family, work, community, love, suffering, or the demands of ordinary life: they "used it all."

Pope Francis urges us "not to get caught up in the details" of the saints' lives, or to suppose that they are somehow flawless. "Not everything a saint says is completely faithful to the Gospel," he says, "not everything he or she does is authentic or perfect. What we need to contemplate is the totality of their life, their entire journey of growth in holiness, the reflection of Jesus Christ that emerges when we grasp their overall meaning as a person" (*GE* 22).

I have often thought that instead of speaking of *saints*, we might better speak of *those who walk the paths of holiness*. All at once we are reminded of everything that connects us with the saints, our fellow travelers, which is much deeper than what sets us apart.[8] We may measure ourselves against great figures like St. Francis, or St. Teresa, or the figures in the stained glass windows, and feel that their witness is beyond anything that can relate to our lives. But their great deeds were often tested in small steps, daily efforts to be more loving and patient.

I think of my own mother, a faithful Episcopalian, though not given much to outward signs of piety. For many years she carried a deep anger toward my father, going back to the time of their divorce many decades before. But at a certain point she let it go. When I asked her how she did that, she said: "I realized I couldn't call myself a Christian unless I could forgive." And I realized that in all those years of going to church, reflecting on the Sunday gospel, she had become one of those followers of Jesus, tagging along, observing his ways, hoping to learn where he was "staying," in hopes that she might stay with him forever.

Still, we may think to ourselves, it would have been so much easier if Jesus had simply provided a guidebook to holiness. Here again our fixation on canonization can distract us from the fact that the saints simply embodied the criteria for holiness that Jesus offered in his Sermon on the Mount, beginning with the Beatitudes, the gospel reading assigned to the feast of All Saints. Pope Francis calls the Beatitudes "a Christian's identity card." He might have called them a Christian's job description.

In the Beatitudes, according to Pope Francis, we find "a portrait of the Master, which we are called to reflect in our daily lives." *Blessed are the poor in spirit . . . Blessed are the meek . . . those who mourn . . . the pure of heart . . . those who hunger and thirst for righteousness . . . the merciful . . . the peacemaker . . . those who are persecuted for righteousness' sake.* Though these "blessings" do not exactly describe the traditional criteria for canonization, we know that when we are in the presence of such people or read their stories, we feel closer to Jesus.

It is not hard to think of holy people from our time who embody these qualities: Mother Teresa (the merciful), Dorothy Day (the peacemaker), Oscar Romero (who hungered and thirsted for righteousness). But if we reflect more deeply, it is also easy to recognize individuals of our own acquaintance, someone such as a teacher, a grandparent, a colleague, a friend. It may be someone who stands out for her gentleness or forgiveness; someone who retains a spirit of joy in the midst of sorrows; someone who risks disapproval or looking foolish for taking an unpopular stand. It may be a husband who lovingly cares for his wife who has Alzheimer's, or parents who love their disabled child; a family that includes the lonely and friendless in their celebrations; someone on whom we can always depend for an example that is loving, brave, and true. Such people, too, represent the face of holiness in our time. It is not likely that they will be canonized. Churches will not be named in their honor. Their images will not be preserved in stained glass windows. And yet they too are among the great cloud of witnesses recognized on the feast of All Saints.

As Pope Francis says, "We are frequently tempted to think that holiness is only for those who can withdraw from ordinary affairs to spend much time in prayer. That is not the case. We are all called to be holy by living our lives with love and by bearing witness in everything we do, wherever we find ourselves" (GE 14).

Wherever we find ourselves, in whatever state of life, the same voice that spoke to the saints also calls to us. We may not follow as far as they did. We may take just the first small steps. The only question is: When we hear that call, how will we answer?

2

READING GOD'S STORY

AT THE TIME OF HIS ORDINATION, in 1969, Jorge Bergoglio—today better known as Pope Francis—wrote this personal "credo":

> I want to believe in God the Father, who loves me like a child, and in Jesus, the Lord, who infused my life with his Spirit, to make me smile and so carry me to the eternal Kingdom of life.
>
> I believe in the church.
>
> I believe in my life story, which was pierced by God's loving gaze, who on that spring day of September 21, came out to meet me to invite me to follow Him.
>
> I believe in my pain, made fruitless by the egotism in which I take refuge.
>
> I believe in the stinginess of my soul, which seeks to take without giving.
>
> I believe in the goodness of others, and that I must love them without fear and without betraying them, never seeking my own security.
>
> I believe in the religious life.
>
> I believe I wish to love a lot.
>
> I believe in the burning death of each day, from which I flee but which smiles at me, inviting me to accept her.
>
> I believe in God's patience, as good and welcoming as a summer's night.
>
> I believe that Dad is with the Lord in heaven...
>
> I believe in Mary, my Mother, who loves me and will never leave me alone.

*And I believe in the surprise of each day, in which
will be manifest love, strength, betrayal, and sin, which
will be always with me until that definitive encounter
with that marvelous face which I do not know, which
always escapes me, but which I wish to know and love.
Amen.*[1]

It is a fascinating and moving document, bearing the strong imprint of the author's Jesuit formation. The Spiritual Exercises of St. Ignatius give special attention to *discernment,* a practice that fosters attention to how God speaks to us in the events of our daily lives, in our life-situation, in the movements of our hearts. It is a discipline aimed at self-knowledge —specifically, regarding the question of our vocation, or how we are meant to serve God's mission.

The young Pope Francis, Jorge Bergoglio

Bergoglio's "creed" is not just a recital of dogmatic truths; it is an affirmation of God's presence in his life. It involves memory, with specific reference to a critical turning point in his life: *"I believe in my life story, which was pierced by God's loving gaze, who on that spring day of September 21, came out to meet me to invite me to follow Him."* He is referring here to the day when he was sixteen years old and happened to walk into a church in Buenos Aires, where he was moved to make his confession and afterward had the burning conviction that he would become a priest.

But while looking back, he also looks toward the future—the promise of his encounter one day with the "marvelous face" of God. And in between there is the present moment—*the surprise of each day*—in which he contends with the struggle between his own weaknesses (his egotism, his stinginess of soul), and his desire "to love a lot."

For Pope Francis, his sense of mission is rooted in a deep apprehension of God's presence in his own life: "*I believe in my life story.*" His life story is part of his creed, along with God, Jesus, Mary, the church, his religious life as a Jesuit. It is a story marked by particular events and relationships, specific joys and sorrows, while it continues to be a story written in the "surprise of every day."

His text invites us to consider how we might compose our own creed, interweaving the articles of faith with an understanding of our own lives and our personal mission. What would it mean to say, "*I believe in my life story*"? Could we also imagine the ways that God is speaking to us—and perhaps to others in ways we cannot know—precisely through our life story?

FOR CHRISTIANS, the notion that God speaks through stories is obvious. The claims of Christianity are staked on a particular story, recounted in the four gospels. When we say that it is a story, we mean that it has a narrative structure. The message is not just revealed in the last chapter, or in some parting words; it emerges through the whole story. And that story is not just an account of miracles or Glorious Mysteries; it is also a story of conflict, rejection, betrayal, and Passion.

If we ask, "Where is God in that story?" the answer is clear: *in the whole story.* Yes, certainly, God is there in the changing of water into wine, the healing miracles, and the multiplication of loaves and fishes. But God is present also in the misunderstandings, the occasions for exasperation, the experience of dejection and apparent failure.

When we look at the gospel this way it invites us to look at our own story with fresh eyes—to see the patterns of grace and mystery that have run through our lives, not just in the moments when we felt closest to God, but even in the times when the thought of God was distant.

St. Augustine was the first Christian writer to look at his life this way, as a kind of spiritual text that told a story about God. [1]

In his *Confessions*, a book written when he was middle-aged, he looked back over his life in light of its critical turning point: his conversion to the Catholic faith. From this vantage point he was able to discern the presence of God in his own life story—even at the times when the thought of God was farthest from him, even in moments of confusion and sadness. As a young man he had sought happiness in friendship, love, pleasure, status, and learning. But his life was continuously shadowed by sadness and suffering—both his own and the suffering he caused others. Something was missing. And yet he was never truly alone, for "all the while," he wrote, "far above, your mercy hovered faithfully about me." His memoir is a reflection on the "living gospel" written in his own life—and an invitation to others to read their own lives in that same light.

Henri Nouwen, the Dutch priest who spent most of his life in North America and achieved wide fame for his spiritual writings (notwithstanding his own restless search and frequent confusion), often said that to be a Christian is precisely a matter of learning to see and understand our own story in relation to the story of Jesus. This is a matter of measuring our actions not simply according to a checklist of Jesus' teachings but rather according to the pattern of his life. And what does that mean? It certainly doesn't mean imitating the pattern of his life as a carpenter in Nazareth or as an itinerant preacher and miracle worker in Palestine. It means living a life in which our own struggles and sufferings, our own efforts to be more loving, more open, more self-giving, find their meaning in his life. That is what it means to walk the path of holiness—which St. Paul described as "putting off the old person and putting on Christ."

Where do we find the meaning of such a life story? Is it on the last page or in the wisdom of a deathbed utterance? I think it is found in the story itself—a story that is not just about moments of religious exaltation but that is also about loneliness, the restless search for a vocation, the experience of misunderstanding and failure, and the will to persevere in the face of all that and more.

In the lives of the saints we see continuously replayed a process by which a person's life story is conformed to, or grafted into, the wider pattern of God's story in Jesus. This happens in countless forms, in greatly differing circumstances, and with allowance for vastly different "human material."

AMONG ALL THE SAINTS IN HISTORY, Francis of Assisi is probably the most influential and beloved. His message is not easily reduced to a set of Franciscan "teachings." Instead, his influence and legacy are rooted more in the example of a way of living—an effort to follow Jesus by imitating *his* way of life, in the form of detachment from worldly values and definitions of success, in a spirit of poverty, in service to and solidarity with the poor and marginalized, and in joyous love for God and all God's creation. His message was shared not so much through his limited writings as through the early biographies and legends that circulated about his life.

St. Francis of Assisi

One of those sources was *The Little Flowers of St. Francis,* a book I happened to discover in the tenth grade while perusing the shelves of my school library. It was a very old book, which allowed me to suppose that I had discovered some kind of buried treasure. I found myself captivated by the picture of a man who tried faithfully, as the author put it, to be "conformed to Christ in all the acts of his life." Here are some of the chapter titles from *The Little Flowers of St. Francis*:

How while St. Francis was talking about God with his companions, Christ appeared among them.

How St. Francis tamed the very fierce wolf of Gubbio.

How St. Francis taught Brother Leo that perfect joy is only in the Cross.

How St. Francis was very kindly received in a home.

How St. Francis freed some doves and made nests for them.

When I told one of my teachers about what I was learning (still somewhat unsure of whether St. Francis was a really famous person), he said, "You don't really believe all that stuff, do you?" I'm not certain whether I answered in words, but my heart was saying, "Yes!"

That reaction echoed the response of many of Francis's contemporaries—not just the young men and women of Assisi who flocked to his side but people of all states of life, including princes and princesses across Europe who were caught up by Franciscan fever. Here was a man who seemed to have discovered the path to heaven, and others wanted to learn his secret.[2]

The best-known stories about St. Francis begin with the account of his conversion, which occurred over a series of episodes. The son of a wealthy cloth merchant, Francis had started out as a carefree reveler who liked to entertain his friends with songs and poetry. His transformation began following his participation in an inglorious military campaign against a neighboring city state. During his recovery from captivity and a subsequent illness, he took to wandering the outskirts of the city, questioning many of his old assumptions about life. One day he encountered a poor leper on the road. After dismounting from his horse, he offered the poor man a few coins. But then, moved by some divine impulse, he leaned forward to kiss the leper's ravaged hands. Francis had always been a fastidious person, with an abhorrence of squalor and illness. But in this gesture he was seemingly liberated from an identity based on status, security, and worldly success. His life began to take shape around an utterly new agenda contrary to the values of his family and his world.

There followed the moment when Francis's father dragged him into town, presented him to the bishop, and accused him of having stolen from his warehouse to provide alms for the poor. Francis admitted his fault and restored his father's money. But then, in an extraordinary gesture, he stripped off his rich garments and handed them also to his sorrowing father, saying, "Hitherto I have called you father on earth; but now I say, 'Our Father, who art in heaven.'"

Finally, there was the moment when he was praying before a crucifix in the dilapidated chapel of San Damiano and heard a voice speak to him: "Francis, repair my church, which has fallen into disrepair, as you can see." At first inclined to take this assignment literally, he set about physically restoring the ruined building. Only later did he understand his mission in a wider, more spiritual sense. His vocation was to recall the church to the radical simplicity of the gospel, to the spirit of poverty and the image of Christ in the poor.

The basic themes of Francis's vision were established in this story. There followed the gathering of his band of brothers, and, with the arrival of Clare of Assisi, the formation of a female branch of the Franciscan family. There are the stories of his preaching to birds, his taming of a fierce wolf in Gubbio, his daring effort to cross the battle lines of the Crusades to meet personally with the Sultan. There are also the stories of his terrible physical sufferings, culminating in his receiving on his hands and feet the very marks of Christ's Passion, his exultant composition of his Canticle to the Creatures, and finally, as he lay naked on the bare ground, his final passage from this life.

Francis's "teachings" were simply based on the Sermon the Mount. His powerful appeal resulted from his demonstrating that these teachings could actually be *lived*. Those who encountered Francis could no longer maintain that Christ's teachings were wonderful in theory but impossible to put into practice. And, in the centuries that followed, the basic reference point for the Franciscan family would always begin with his story.

In Francis, we see the grafting of one person's biography into the story of Jesus. It is possible to read the lives of many other saints in a similar light.

I GREW UP in an Episcopal parish named for St. Alban, the first martyr of the English church. I don't recall ever hearing a sermon about St. Alban, whom I presumed to be some sort of English bishop from long ago. It was only many years later that I read his story and learned that he lived in Roman-occupied Britain during the third century. At the time of an outbreak of persecution against Christians, Alban gave shelter to a priest who was on the run. Although Alban was a non-Christian, he was touched by the faith of his guest, and after several days he asked to receive instruction and was baptized. Aware that soldiers were in close pursuit, Alban contrived to help the priest escape by exchanging clothes with him. When the soldiers arrived at his house, they arrested Alban in place of the priest and brought him before a judge, whereupon he declared himself a Christian. Accepting the punishment intended for the priest he had impersonated, Alban was flogged and ultimately beheaded.[3]

In discovering this remarkable story, I was deeply moved. At the same time I felt cheated for never having heard any of this as I grew up and worshiped in St. Alban's Church. It would have supplied an example of what I craved—a sense of the heroic, an example of what Bonhoeffer called "the cost of discipleship." And here in the very name of my parish church was the subversive memory of a Christian who laid down his life, who heroically fulfilled the duties of compassion and solidarity with his persecuted neighbor. In assuming the clothing of a persecuted outlaw, Alban—a newly baptized Christian—quite vividly put on Christ, with all the consequences that that entailed. With his deeds and sacrifice he wrote a living gospel.

PROBABLY MOST HOLY MEN AND WOMEN could identify with the spirit of Pope Francis's creed when he wrote, "I believe in my life story." Some, following the example of St. Augustine, wrote their own spiritual autobiographies, or recalled a particular occasion when they felt themselves "pierced by God's loving gaze, who...came out to meet me to invite me to follow."

There is St. Ignatius of Loyola, the founder of the Society of Jesus, who spent his early life as a soldier and courtier. One day in battle he suffered a grievous injury when his leg was shattered by a cannon ball. In the months of his recovery, he asked for something to read—preferably tales of courtly honor. Instead he was given a book of lives of the saints. As he became increasingly drawn into these stories, he found that thoughts of his previous life brought him feelings of "desolation." In contrast, as he imagined what it would be like to live like St. Francis or St. Dominic, he experienced a sense of "consolation." Upon his recovery, he went on pilgrimage, laid his sword and armor on the altar in a chapel of the Blessed Mother, and vowed to become a "soldier of Christ."[4]

There is the story of St. Teresa of Calcutta, an Albanian nun, who spent twenty years of her life teaching in one of her order's schools in India. One day, while traveling on a train to Darjeeling, she received an unmistakable call from God "to be poor with the poor," and to love God "in the most distressing disguise of the poorest of the poor." With the permission of her congregation she left her convent, replaced her habit with a simple white sari, and went out to encounter Jesus in the desperate byways of Calcutta. It was the beginning of what would become the Missionaries of Charity, an international order rooted in Mother Teresa's ministry among the dying and in the "call within a call" that she had experienced that day on a train ride in the Himalayas.

In the case of St. Vincent de Paul, who had been a worldly priest serving as personal chaplain to a wealthy French aristocrat, the call to transform his life took place when he was summoned to hear the dying confession of a peasant on his lord's estate. After the man had received absolution, he happened to remark that he might well have perished in a state of mortal sin had the priest not heard his confession. Vincent was struck as never before by the seriousness of his vocation. He determined that from that moment on his priesthood would be dedicated to service of the poor.

Many saints, including St. Ignatius, St. Teresa of Avila, and St. Therese of Lisieux, following the example of St. Augustine, wrote their own spiritual autobiographies. Among their modern counterparts are Thomas Merton and Dorothy Day—both of whom, like Augustine, undertook to examine their lives from the standpoint of their conversion. Merton's story, *The Seven Storey Mountain,* culminated with his becoming a Trappist monk, while Day's memoir, *The Long Loneliness,* concluded with the founding and early history of the Catholic Worker movement. In both cases, they told a story marked by joy and love, by fortuitous encounters with books and friends, by intuitions of transcendence, but also by sorrow and loss and long stretches when the thought of God was far away. Ultimately, they came to see it all as a story of grace. God was present in the whole story, both in the lonely wandering in the wilderness and in the experiences of discovery and homecoming.

Dorothy Day wrote two accounts of her conversion. *The Long Loneliness,* published in 1952, was her second draft of the story. In 1938 she had published a shorter version, *From Union Square to Rome.* Like St. Augustine in his *Confessions,* she describes in both versions the succession of events that led her to God. But whereas Augustine tended to wrap most of his early life in a cloud of shame and regret, Day preferred to see everything that she experienced—even her faults and failings—as encompassed by God's grace.

Day grew up in New York, Oakland, and Chicago. Her father was a sportswriter who liked to pepper his columns with references to Shakespeare and the King James Bible, and yet, as she writes, "in the family the name of God was never mentioned."

Dorothy Day with her younger sister Della

Nevertheless, her childhood was marked by intimations of some deeper, transcendent dimension to life, the memory of which would linger. One of these occurred when she was a child living in Chicago and went searching one morning for her friend Kathryn Barrett, who lived in a neighboring tenement building. Bursting into Kathryn's apartment, she was startled to come upon Mrs. Barrett, her friend's mother, on her knees and saying her prayers. Mrs. Barrett calmly informed her that Kathryn was out, and then carried on with her prayers. Day writes, "I felt a warm burst of love toward Mrs. Barrett that I have never forgotten, a feeling of gratitude and happiness that still warms my heart when I remember her. She had God, and there was beauty and joy in her life."[5]

That memory, remarkably, remained with her—even over the course of a life marked by unusual drama, even as she "groaned at the hideous sordidness of man's lot . . . Still there were moments when, in the midst of misery and class strife, life was shot through with glory. Mrs. Barrett in her sordid little tenement flat finished her breakfast dishes at ten o'clock in the morning and got down on her knees and prayed to God." (Pause for a moment to acknowledge this: Behind every great saint there are undoubtedly many other anonymous figures like Mrs. Barrett, who could never conceive the influence of their simple witness.)

While in college, Day adopted a cynical attitude toward religion. "Christ no longer walked the streets of this world. He was two thousand years dead and new prophets had risen up in His place." Now, she says, she "was in love with the masses."[6]

Abandoning college, she moved to New York City and found work with a number of radical journals while otherwise immersing herself in the struggle for social justice. Yet, even after a late night of drinking and smoking in Greenwich Village taverns, something would draw her into an early morning Mass at St. Joseph's Church on Sixth Avenue. Sitting with the people in church, she says, she "seemed to feel the faith of those about me and I longed for their faith." Her own life, she writes, "was sordid, and yet I had had occasional glimpses of the true and the beautiful."[7]

But she also writes of suffering—a brutal experience in jail as a result of her arrest in a women's suffrage protest and a subsequent unexpected arrest in Chicago—which gave her a deep sense of human suffering and of solidarity with all victims of injustice. And there were experiences she couldn't bear to write about, including the tragic love affair that resulted in an abortion, and, apparently, a suicide attempt.[8] Among the many things that brought her to God, Day gives special credit to her experiences in the radical movement. Even after becoming a Catholic, Day was determined not to turn her back on all that was good and noble in these principles: the spirit of solidarity, reverence for the poor and oppressed, respect for the dignity of work, the willingness to suffer for a cause, the spirit of idealism, and the capacity for indignation. In the gospels, all this found a wider reference.

The climax of her first memoir and the turning point of her later version come with the period of peace and joy she experienced while living on Staten Island with Forster Batterham, a man she deeply loved, and the discovery that she was once again pregnant.

Here is another place where Day's "confessions" depart from the model of St. Augustine—one of the few saints to have acknowledged any kind of sexual history. Augustine writes at length about his youthful search for "some object for my love." In different forms and persons, including his mistress of many years, he evidently found it. But in every case Augustine wants to show how the "clear waters" of love were invariably spoiled by the "black rivers of lust." He describes his relationship with his unnamed mistress, the mother of his son, in these unflattering

terms: "In those days I lived with a woman, not my lawful wedded wife, but a mistress whom I had chosen for no special reason
but that my restless passions had alighted on her."[9]

It is striking to compare Augustine's treatment with a similar
passage in *The Long Loneliness,* in which Day introduces the
story of her love affair with Forster and the role he played in hastening her spiritual journey: "The man I loved, with whom I entered into a common-law marriage, was an anarchist, an
Englishman by descent, and a biologist."[10] They had met at a
party in Greenwich Village in the early 1920s and soon thereafter
began to live together—as she put it, "in the fullest sense of the
phrase"—in a cottage on Staten Island.

In their bohemian set there was nothing scandalous about
such a relationship. It was evidently Dorothy who liked to think
of it as a "common-law marriage." For Forster, who never
masked his scorn for the "institution of the family," their relationship was simply a "comradeship." Nevertheless, she loved
him "in every way." As she wrote: "I loved him for all he knew
and pitied him for all he didn't know. I loved him for the odds
and ends I had to fish out of his sweater pockets and for the sand
and shells he brought in with his fishing. I loved his lean cold
body as he got into bed smelling of the sea and I loved his integrity and stubborn pride."[11]

Day is here describing, without any hint of Augustine's oblig-
atory shame or regret, her physical relationship with a man "not
her lawful wedded husband." Needless to say, she was not yet a
Catholic. Yet her point is to show how this lesson in love, this
time of "natural happiness," as she called it, awakened her
thirst for an even greater happiness. She began praying during
her walks along the beach, and even attending Mass. This religious impulse was strengthened when she discovered she was
pregnant—an event that inspired a sense of gratitude so large that
only God could receive it. And with that came the determination
that she would have her child baptized, "come what may."

As a dedicated anarchist, Forster would not be married by
either church or state. And so, to become a Catholic, Dorothy

Dorothy Day on Staten Island

realized, would mean separating from the man she loved. "It got to the point where it was the simple question of whether I chose God or man."[12] Ultimately, painfully, she chose God. In December 1927, she forced Forster to leave the house. That month she was received into the church.

Day's conversion is only one critical part of her story. The fundamental question of her vocation had to do with how to reconcile her faith with her commitment to the poor and oppressed. That question was ultimately resolved in the founding of the Catholic Worker, the movement that she launched in 1933 with Peter Maurin and that would become her home for the rest of her life.

Simone Weil wrote an essay on what she called "the implicit forms of the love of God," including friendship, love of neighbor, the beauty of the world, and religious practice.[13] All these, she wrote, have a capacity to elevate the soul, even where God is not explicitly mentioned. All these "implicit" forms are present in Day's story. But in *From Union Square to Rome* she adds another: devotion to the poor and a passion for justice. Quoting the novelist François Mauriac, she writes: "It is impossible for any one of those who has real charity in his heart not to serve Christ. Even some of those who think they hate Him, have consecrated their lives to Him; for Jesus is disguised and masked in the midst of men, hidden among the poor, among the sick, among prisoners, among strangers."[14] In her memoirs she describes the steps by which such implicit love of God became explicit and how she came to accept the faith that was "always in [her] heart."

My father, Daniel Ellsberg, in Vietnam

IN MY OWN LIFE I experienced yet another "implicit form" of the love of God—namely, in the struggle against war and the yearning for peace. My father, Daniel Ellsberg, a defense analyst working for the U.S. government, volunteered in 1965 to go to Vietnam. He left a dedicated Cold Warrior, and he returned two years later utterly disillusioned with the war and determined to help end it. What had largely effected this change was the suffering of the Vietnamese people, who had "become as real to me as my own hands." His anti-war fervor was intensified by his work on a top-secret history of the war, later known as the Pentagon Papers. He was now convinced that the war was not simply a mistake, but a crime in process. After encountering young men who were doing all they could to resist the war simply by refusing to cooperate with the draft and going to jail, he asked himself what he could do to end the war if he were willing to go to jail. The answer occurred to him: he could copy and release the seven-thousand-page history of the war that was sitting in his office safe. And so he did.[15]

Through him I was introduced to the world of dedicated peacemakers, many of them inspired by the teachings of Mohandas Gandhi, who would become my particular hero and guide. One day in October 1969 my father asked me to help him copy the Pentagon Papers. My younger sister joined in, and so we played a small role in a drama we could not fully understand. (I was thirteen.) I know he wanted to impart a sense of what he had learned—that there were causes that were larger than oneself, reasons why one might be called to make sacrifices for the greater good. And this implanted in me the conviction that I must find my own higher purpose and calling in life.

My parents divorced when I was eight, and I grew up with my mother, a faithful Episcopalian. I liked going to church, where I served as an acolyte and sang in the choir. I also liked to approach the rector after services and offer my critique of his sermons (which he surely appreciated!). I didn't learn much about saints—even those who adorned the stained glass windows of our church—but we sang hymns about them: those who were "patient and brave and true," who "toiled and fought and lived and died for the Lord they loved and knew." But I didn't think I knew any people like that—despite the assurance that there were still hundreds and thousands of them all around us: "You can meet them in school, or in lanes, or at sea / in church, or in trains, or in shops, or at tea."

By the time I was in college I had become detached from any practical connection to the church. New heroes in the struggle for peace and justice had taken the place of the figures in stained glass windows. I felt a deep hunger to pursue questions for which I could find no answer in college. My mother watched with growing apprehension. Communication became strained. When, after my sophomore year, I told her I was leaving Harvard, she thought I was making a terrible mistake, and her disappointment was severe.

The day I planned to set out on my great adventure into the unknown, she left for work without saying a word, and I wondered if that would spell the future of our relationship and whether we would ever truly communicate about what was important to me and what I was seeking.

But that same morning my mother called me from work. I will always remember that call. She said, "I realize that what we want for our children is that they be safe and happy"—"mindlessly happy," I think she put it. "But," she said, "that is not what we want for ourselves. We want to find our own way—to have a life that is meaningful, to take risks, to fall and get back up again and learn everything we can. So you do that. You go with my blessings and find everything you are looking for."

What I sought and discovered is largely reflected in the stories and the people described in the chapters that follow, beginning with the Catholic Worker, a fortuitous first stop on my journey, where I found myself detained for the next five years. In a sense I never left.

In one of the last columns she wrote, Dorothy Day described the function of the Catholic Worker: "It is, in a way, a school, a work camp, to which large-hearted, socially conscious young people come to find their vocations. After some months or years, they know most definitely what they want to do with their lives. Some go into medicine, nursing, law, teaching, farming, writing, and publishing [!]. They learn not only to love, with compassion, but to overcome fear, that dangerous emotion that precipitates violence."[16]

Some lessons are never finished.

In telling the stories of saints and holy people, it can sometimes seem that they are no more than a catalog of pious attitudes and heroic achievements. The more interesting accounts enable us to read the story of God that is written in their lives. That "living gospel" is reflected not just in their accomplishments, but in their search, in their ongoing struggle to be faithful, and in the full expression of their humanity. Their holiness is a quality expressed in the process of their life, in their total response, over a lifetime, to the divine voice that called them deeper into the heart of their vocation. To tell the story of holy people means reading their story in the light of the gospel and endeavoring to discern how their life relates to the story that God is telling us through Jesus—the one, as the pope says, who infused their life with his Spirit, to make them smile and so to carry them to eternal life.

That is a story that also takes account of their stumbling, their moments of doubt, the "pain, made fruitless by the egotism in which [they] take refuge," their experience of "the goodness of others," as well as "the burning death of each day." And if we ask, "Where is God in that story?" the answer is that God is present in the whole story. And whether we realize it or not, the same is true for us.

DOROTHY DAY
A Pilgrim

ON MAY 1, 1933, at a Communist rally in Union Square in New York City, Dorothy Day and a small troupe of followers distributed the first issue of the *Catholic Worker* newspaper. She described its purpose in her first editorial, which was written, along with the rest of the paper, at her kitchen table:

> For those who are sitting on park benches in the warm spring sunlight. For those who are huddling in shelters trying to escape the rain. For those who are walking the streets in the all but futile search for work. For those who think that there is no hope for the future, no recognition of their plight—this little paper is addressed.
>
> It is printed to call their attention to the fact that the Catholic Church has a social program—to let them know that there are men of God who are working not only for their spiritual but for their material welfare.[1]

She had sought no permission or authorization from the hierarchy before launching this paper. She had no clerical advisor or board of directors. She herself was a convert of only six years, an

This chapter is adapted from a presentation at Oblate School of Theology, San Antonio, TX, October 30, 2015, "Dorothy Day for Today Conference," which was published in revised form as "Dorothy Day: A Saint for Our Time" in *Spiritus: A Journal of Christian Spirituality* 16, no. 1 (2016).

unwed, single mother, with fairly limited Catholic contacts and little theological formation beyond her reading of scripture, the Baltimore Catechism, and the lives of the saints. And yet, in the midst of the Great Depression, she perceived the need for a new Catholic voice, one that would relate the gospel to the plight of the poor and the struggle for social justice, and she undertook on her own initiative to provide that voice.

Distributing the first issue of the Catholic Worker, May 1, 1933

By the time of her death, nearly fifty years later, Dorothy Day was widely regarded as the radical conscience of the American Catholic Church. Historian David O'Brien, in an obituary for *Commonweal*, described her as "the most important, interesting, and influential figure in the history of American Catholicism"— a statement that has suddenly become even more plausible in light of Pope Francis's surprising decision to cite her among the four great Americans he held up as moral beacons.[2] But it was not always so. For most of Day's life she was a fairly marginal figure— far outside the mainstream, operating without any official support or recognition from the church hierarchy, unfamiliar to most readers of the Catholic press. No Catholic bishop attended her funeral.

As a convert to Catholicism, she remained quite traditional in her religious practice. She attended Mass each day. As a Benedictine oblate she prayed from a breviary, and she was never without her rosary. She was steeped in the lives of the saints and her everyday speech and writing were filled with references to figures like St. Augustine, St. Teresa of Avila, and St. Francis of Assisi.

And yet there was something quite different about her—different from almost anyone who came before—because she consciously combined her traditional faith with a radical approach to social and political issues. It was a conjunction of attitudes that didn't really exist before Dorothy Day came along. Together with other radicals she marched in demonstrations, walked on picket lines, and was regularly arrested for acts of civil disobedience—the last time when she was seventy-five.

Like many of the saints she revered, she spent her life in active service to the poor. But she didn't stop with charity and the works of mercy. She joined the practice of charity with a passion for social justice. She believed it was not enough to feed the poor, but that we must ask why they are poor; we must analyze and expose and resist those structures and institutional forces that give rise to poverty and the need for so much charity.

The *Catholic Worker* was the name of her newspaper, which sells today as it did more than eighty-five years ago for "a penny a copy." The Catholic Worker is also the name of a lay Catholic movement that has attempted to show how the radical gospel commandment of love can be lived.

Some people called her a communist. Such criticism didn't bother her much. She liked to say that it was the complacency of Christians, in her youth, that had made her love the communists, and it was the communists, in turn, with their love of the poor, who had led her to Christ.

For his part, J. Edgar Hoover, Director of the FBI, said of her:

Dorothy Day is a very erratic and irresponsible person. She has engaged in activities, which strongly suggest that she is consciously or unconsciously being used by communist groups. From past experience with her it is obvious she maintains a very hostile and belligerent attitude toward the Bureau and makes every effort to castigate the FBI whenever she feels so inclined.[3]

(When I read this to her she was delighted: "They make me sound like a mean, old woman," she said. "Read it again!")

When Dorothy's cause for canonization was endorsed by the U.S. bishops some years ago, a state senator from Virginia wrote to Pope Benedict to say he was "revolted" by the thought that a person of such "loathsome character" might be considered a saint.

She took criticism like this in stride. On the other hand, many people also called her a saint. That was another matter. "Don't call me a saint," she was quoted as saying. "I don't want to be dismissed that easily." When I say "she was quoted," I may well mean, "she was quoted by me." I used this line in 1984 in the introduction to my edition of her selected writings. I have no recollection of the original source. And yet I am constantly surprised to discover that it is the one line of Dorothy's that everyone seems to know. It is even the title of a documentary about her. I have some regrets about this. It gives the impression that Dorothy was cynical about the naming and veneration of saints—which couldn't be farther from the truth. What Dorothy opposed—and what actual saint wouldn't?—was being put on a pedestal, fitted to some preconceived model of holiness that would strip her of her humanity and, at the same time, blunt the radical challenge of the gospel.

After all, people might say: "Dorothy Day could do such things (live in poverty, feed the hungry, or go to jail for the cause of peace) because, after all, she's a saint," the implication being that such actions—which would be unthinkable for normal people—must have come easily for her. But nothing came easily for Dorothy. As she said of her vocation, "Neither revolutions nor faith is won without keen suffering. For me Christ was not to be bought for thirty pieces of silver but with my heart's blood."[4]

Of course, if she is eventually named Saint Dorothy, she will be a saint with an unusual backstory—having renounced Christianity in her youth and spent her early years as a journalist and activist for radical causes. Among canonized saints, she would perhaps be unique for having been arrested for acts of civil disobedience; her first arrest was for having picketed in front of the White House on behalf of women's suffrage, and it resulted in a thirty-day jail sentence in the Occoquan workhouse in Virginia.

Her friends were anarchists, communists, and assorted literary bohemians, including Mike Gold, later editor of the Communist *Daily Worker*, and the playwright Eugene O'Neill. In the aftermath of an unhappy love affair she had an abortion. This is hardly the standard fare of *Butler's Lives of the Saints*. And yet there was always in Dorothy some yearning for the transcendent. Like a character in Dostoevsky, she observed, "All my life I have been haunted by God."[5]

Yet even the circumstances of her conversion were unusual—in fact, unique in the annals of the saints—prompted by the experience of pregnancy and the birth of her daughter. This occurred while she was living on Staten Island with a man she deeply loved, Forster Batterham. After years of strife and unhappiness, this experience of love and what she called "natural happiness" turned her heart to the possibility of "a greater happiness to be obtained from life than any I had ever known." She writes: "I began to think, to weigh things more, and it was at this time that I began consciously to pray more."[6]

It was also at this time that Dorothy discovered she was pregnant. This event had enormous significance for her. Following her earlier abortion she had believed she couldn't have children. Now she experienced an impulse of gratitude so large that only God could receive it. And "with this came the need to worship, to adore."[7] She decided that she would have her child baptized in the Catholic Church, "cost what it may." The cost was great. She knew that "Forster would have nothing to do with religion or with me, if I embraced it."[8] The real issue was marriage; Forster, a dedicated anarchist, would have nothing to do with it.

Dorothy Day and her daughter Tamar

BUT THERE WAS ANOTHER SENSE OF LOSS, as well. Her steady gravitation toward the Catholic Church also seemed, initially, to involve a painful betrayal of the working class. She believed the Catholic Church was the church of the poor. As her father put it, it was the church of "Irish cops and washerwomen." That was part of its attraction. But to her radical friends—and, sadly, to her as well—it seemed more like a friend of the rich, the ultimate defender of the status quo. Dorothy knew nothing of Catholic social teaching, a term she was unlikely to hear in any typical Sunday sermon.

She was literally at a loss as to how she might reconcile her faith and her loyalty to the cause of the oppressed. After her baptism in 1927, followed immediately by her separation from Forster, she spent the next five years in a kind of wilderness, praying to find some way of reconciling these two halves of her soul.

The seeds of this dilemma went back much farther. Even as a young person Dorothy recognized the need for a new type of saint. In her autobiography, *The Long Loneliness*, she describes her first childhood encounters with the lives of the saints, recalling how her heart was stirred by stories of their charity toward the sick, the maimed, the lepers. "But there was another question in my mind," she said. "Why was so much done in remedying the evil instead of avoiding it in the first place? . . . Where were the saints to try to change the social order, not just to minister to the slaves, but to do away with slavery?"[9]

In effect, Dorothy's vocation took form around this challenge. Her conversion to Catholicism and her work in founding the Catholic Worker movement would come many years later. But the great underlying mission of her life was to join the practice of charity with the struggle for justice—thereby inventing a model of holiness that had never before existed. Because of Dorothy, future generations of Christians would not have to ask her question—Where are the saints to try to change the social order? It was a question she answered with her own life.

Meanwhile, the search for this path took her in December 1932 to Washington to cover a "Hunger March of the Unemployed." As she watched the ragged parade of men, led by many of her old communist comrades, she asked herself why Catholics weren't leading such a march. The question led her to the Shrine of the Immaculate Conception. As this was actually on December 8, the Feast of the Immaculate Conception, there could not have been a more auspicious setting. There she offered up a prayer "with tears and anguish" that "some way would open up for me to use what talents I possessed for my fellow workers, for the poor." She longed, as she put it, "to make a synthesis reconciling body and soul, this world and the next."[10]

When she returned to New York she found Peter Maurin waiting for her in her apartment. In that encounter, though it took a while for her to realize it, her prayer was answered. And in the Catholic Worker movement that ensued she found the synthesis she had been seeking.

Peter Maurin was a French immigrant of peasant origins, twenty years her senior. He had spent many years tramping around the country, devising a philosophy aimed at unleashing the radical social implications of the gospel and looking for someone to help set his ideas into motion.

His philosophy was expressed in what he came to call "Easy Essays"—short, phrased essays ideal for street-corner declamation. For example:

The world would become better off
if people tried to become better.
And people would become better
If they stopped trying to become better off.[11]

Peter Maurin's first gift to Dorothy was a "Catholic view of history" and a personalist philosophy to replace the class-struggle approach of her radical past. "The future will be different," he proclaimed, "if we make the present different."[12] But before meeting Dorothy Day, he seems to have been singularly incapable of translating his abstract ideas into action on a scale larger than himself. One of the problems was his thick French accent. He compensated by discovering a way of non-stop talking, seemingly without the necessity of taking a breath. His suit looked as if he had slept in it—as indeed he had. And he never bathed. Asked why he didn't take more care of his appearance, he answered, "So as not to arouse envy." Even Dorothy acknowledged that for a long time she was not sure whether she really liked him. Nevertheless. she revered him as a saint and always credited him as the true founder of the Catholic Worker. Perhaps one of Peter Maurin's major contributions was simply to give Dorothy "permission" to launch her own movement. Drawing on the lives of the saints, he showed that it was not necessary to wait for anyone to authorize or sponsor the way of discipleship. The saints began immediately with whatever means were at hand. If God blessed their venture the means would arrive.

For Dorothy this meant launching her newspaper with no money; calling it the *Catholic Worker* without seeking prior permission from the bishop or any other authority, and daring to offer a "Catholic" perspective on social issues of the day that was far in advance of contemporary social teaching.

Rather than just agitate about social injustice, articles in the *Catholic Worker* described what society would look like if it were organized around values of solidarity, community, and human dignity instead of selfishness and greed. Dorothy and Peter believed it was not enough to write about these ideas; they had to live them out. This led to the formation of "houses of hospitality" for the practice of the works of mercy and soup kitchens where the hungry could be fed. Those who joined the work lived in community, in voluntary poverty, among the poor they served. At the same time, Dorothy believed that just caring for the poor was not enough; it was also necessary to challenge, protest, and resist the structures that caused such poverty and the need for charity—particularly the spirit of financial speculation, the valuation of capital and property over labor, and the diversion of resources to militarism.

Many people—conservative and liberal alike—were confounded by Dorothy's ability to integrate a traditional style of Catholic piety with a radical style of social engagement. But in her eyes there was no paradox. The basis of the synthesis she had been seeking was found in the central doctrine of her faith: the Incarnation. Her mission was rooted in the radical social implications of this doctrine: the fact that, in Christ, God had entered our humanity and our history, so that all creation was hallowed, and whatever we did for our neighbors we did directly for him. This was the bedrock teaching of Jesus: "I was hungry, and you fed me, thirsty and you gave me a drink... Insofar as you did these things for the least of my brothers and sisters, you did them for me."

In the very doctrine of the Incarnation Dorothy found the synthesis she had been seeking: the way to reconcile "body and soul," the spiritual and the material, the historical and the transcendent, the love of God and the love of neighbor, "this world and the next."

When Dorothy spoke of the real presence of Christ in the poor, many people accepted this, even applauding what they called her "wonderful work for the poor." Things became more controversial when she extended this principle to solidarity with the labor movement and a general critique of the capitalist system. But when she applied this logic to the problem of war and violence, that was another matter entirely. Yet she followed the same logic all the way. Christ was present in the disguise of our neighbor—even in his most terrible disguise, in the face of the one we call the enemy.

Her pacifism, expressed first during the Spanish Civil War, maintained throughout World War II, and continued in the era of the Cold War and Vietnam, caused outrage and scandal—even among many who admired her work with the poor.

In the January 1942 issue of the *Catholic Worker*, following the attack on Pearl Harbor, she shared her anguished prayer: "Lord God, merciful God, our Father, shall we keep silent or shall we speak? And if we speak, what shall we say?" Answering her own questions, she wrote: "We will print the words of Christ who is with us always—even to the end of the world... Love your enemies, do good to those who hate you." Her manifesto, she declared, was the Sermon on the Mount.[13]

Nevertheless, the movement was bitterly divided. Many of her closest supporters parted ways with her. Subscriptions to the paper plummeted. Yet she believed that even in the case of an apparently just cause, a remnant must cling to the possibility of a different way. The alternative, the logic of violence, she believed, led inevitably to the fire-bombing of Tokyo, the atomic bombs, and the possibility of global annihilation.

No doubt her position was true folly in the eyes of the world. But we were not told to love within the limits of reason, prudence, or personal safety— but to love unreasonably, foolishly, profligately, even unto death on the Cross. In the era of nuclear weapons, she believed, the teaching of indiscriminate love had become a practical necessity, an imperative. To live under the canopy of such weapons without resisting, without raising an outcry, was, in her view, to participate in the ultimate blasphemy.

Dorothy Day:
Loving beyond the limits of reason

Beginning in the 1950s the Catholic Worker sponsored numerous protests against nuclear war. For her own refusal to cooperate with New York City's compulsory civil defense drills, Dorothy served several jail terms. Most Catholic leaders of the time probably considered her refusal to be a foolish gesture. This was at a time when supposedly sane members of the political and military establishment were prepared to imagine victory in a war that could claim hundreds of millions of lives. In relation to such thinking, Dorothy did not mind being considered foolish, impractical, or even crazy. From her point of view, policies that were considered prudent, practical, and sane were in fact murderous, suicidal, and blasphemous! And yet, I'm not aware that any American bishop of that time spoke out in her defense. Certainly none joined her in jail.

Dorothy did not expect great things to happen overnight. She knew the slow pace by which change and new life comes. It was, in the phrase she often repeated, "by little and by little" that we were saved.

And yet she acted out of deep faith in the mystical bonds of cause and effect in which we are all connected. Any act of love might contribute to the balance of love in the world, any suffering endured in love might ease the burden of others. We could only make use of the little things we possessed—the little faith, the little strength, the little courage. These were the loaves and fishes. We could only offer what we had and pray that God would make the increase.

TO HAVE KNOWN DOROTHY DAY, as her granddaughter Kate Hennessy has said, "means spending the rest of your life wondering what hit you."[14] That is certainly the case for me. I first met Dorothy in the summer of 1975, when I was nineteen. I had dropped out of college after my sophomore year and made my way to St. Joseph's, the Catholic Worker community on the Lower East Side of Manhattan. A number of motivations drew me. I was eager to experience something of life firsthand, not just from books. I was tired of living for myself alone and longed to give myself to something larger and more meaningful. I had intended to stay just a few months, but that turned into five years—the last five years, as it turned out, of Dorothy's life. And in the end, I found much of what I had been seeking—and perhaps much more.

I remember our first encounter. Dwight Macdonald, in a famous *New Yorker* profile, once compared Dorothy to "an elderly schoolteacher or librarian; she has the typical air of mild authority and of being no longer surprised at anything children or book-borrowers may do."[15] Naturally, I was apprehensive. Knowing the importance of first impressions, I had spent a lot of time preparing to ask just the right question. But when the moment came, all I could do was blurt out, "How do you reconcile Catholicism and anarchism?" She looked at me with a bemused expression I would come to know well, and said, "It's never been a problem for me."

Lacking a follow-up question, I had no choice but to withdraw and ponder her answer, wondering if it contained some deeper Zen meaning.

Over time I came to realize the truth: that Dorothy had little interest in abstractions. The real question for Dorothy was how ideals were lived out and set in motion. She would have been much more interested if I had asked her a question about Tolstoy or Sacco and Vanzetti. And by the same token she was fascinated by other people and their stories, where they came from, where they had traveled, what books they liked. "What's your favorite novel by Dostoevsky?" she might ask. It wasn't a test; she was genuinely curious. And it turned out she was not hard to get to know—especially if you weren't overly reverent. She thrived on conversations over a cup of coffee or around the kitchen table. She had a sly sense of humor and an almost girlish laugh. People are surprised to hear that, because in photos she almost always looked severe and intimidating.

A few months after my arrival Dorothy asked me to become the managing editor of the paper. She was, as she liked to say, "in retirement," and the day-to-day management of the paper and the household was in the hands of those she called "the young people." At twenty, I certainly qualified as young. Otherwise, I had no other obvious qualifications. I

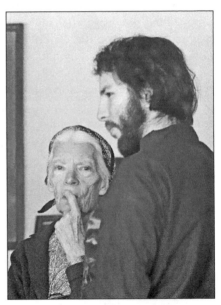

During one of my conversations with Dorothy

wasn't even a Catholic. My selection evidently had more to do with the fact that no one else was particularly interested in the job. Nevertheless, Dorothy had faith in people, and she was able to make them feel her faith as well; she had an uncanny ability to discern and encourage people's hidden gifts and talents. (I could scarcely imagine at the time that she was pointing me in the direction of my life's work and vocation.)

She didn't always endorse my editorial decisions—especially if the articles were too long, or my tone was too sarcastic, or the illustrations were too lugubrious. The only instruction I can recall was the time she told me: "Your job as editor is to make sure I don't sound like a fool." (It was the least challenging aspect of the job.)

Life at the Catholic Worker involved constant improvisation. One day it might involve getting up early to help prepare for the morning "line"—the hundred or so down-and-out men and women who showed up each day, rain or shine, for a bowl of soup, some bread and tea. It might involve adjudicating a dispute between unruly guests in the house of hospitality, or welcoming visitors, or folding newspapers to be mailed across the country, or begging for vegetables at the wholesale market, or cleaning one of the regularly clogged toilets (my talents were not in this area). But it might also involve handing out antiwar leaflets to indifferent crowds on Fifth Avenue, marching in demonstrations, or a sit-in at the Pentagon. You never knew. As for Dorothy, she answered mail, said her prayers, attended daily Mass at the local parish when she was able, and joined the community at the end of the day in reciting Evening Prayers.

DOROTHY SPENT MOST OF HER LIFE among the down and out, among the sights and smells of poverty, eating plain and often ill-prepared food, contending with bed bugs and lice, constantly worrying about whether the morning's mail would bring in enough to keep the lights on or cover the cost of beans. On so many occasions she contended with "drunkenness, madness, filth and ugliness."[16] In light of this reality, I was surprised to discover her fastidious nature and her cultivated tastes: she loved classical music, the opera, literature, flowers, and beautiful things. She covered the walls of her room in Maryhouse, the shelter for homeless women she opened in her last years, with postcards: icons and paintings, but also pictures of nature—forests, the ocean, icebergs. (One time when I was in jail she sent me one of these postcards— an aerial photo of Cape Cod with the inscription, "I hope this card refreshes you and does not tantalize you.") She loved to quote Dostoevsky's words, "The world will be saved by beauty."

And for all the sadness and suffering that surrounded her, she never lacked an eye for the transcendent. There were always moments when it was possible to see beneath the surface. "Just look at that tree!" she would say. Or it might be some act of kindness, or the opera on the radio, or some vines climbing the fire escape in the middle of a slum. Moments like that made her want to rejoice. She liked to quote St. Teresa of Avila, who said, "I am such a grateful person that I can be purchased with a sardine."

There is a famous story about the time someone donated a diamond ring to the Catholic Worker. Everyone wondered what Dorothy would do with it. It would have paid for a lot of beans! She gave it to an old woman who used to hang around the Worker—a woman so disagreeable that she had earned the nickname "the Weasel." When it was pointed out that that ring could cover this woman's rent for most of a year, Dorothy said she could do with it what she wanted: use it for rent, take a trip to the Bahamas, or keep it to admire. She said, "Do you suppose God created diamonds only for the rich?"

When I heard that story I recognized that distinctive audacity or over-the-top extravagance that distinguishes holiness from just being especially nice—whether it is St. Francis kissing a leper, or the woman who wasted a large quantity of expensive oil anointing Christ's feet. In the realm of Dorothy's social activism, it has its analogue in her reply to an exasperated IRS agent who asked her to estimate how much federal income tax she thought she owed: "Why don't you just figure out how much I owe, then you tell me, and then I just won't pay it."

I had the privilege of spending a number of years editing Dorothy Day's personal papers, including her diaries, *The Duty of Delight*, and her letters, *All the Way to Heaven*. The phrase, "the duty of delight," was one of Dorothy's favorites. She found it in a letter by the English critic John Ruskin. It recurs throughout her diaries so often as to become a kind of mantra, often following a recital of drudgery or disappointment. It served as a reminder to find God in all things—the sorrows of daily life as well as the moments of joy, both of which she experienced in abundance.

As familiar as I thought I was with Dorothy's life and writings, working with her personal papers revealed dimensions of her humanity that came as a revelation. In her letters the most astonishing discovery was the three-dozen letters to Forster Batterham, the father of her daughter, the man she liked to call her "common-law husband." These letters date from the beginning of their romance in 1925 until the eve of her meeting with Peter Maurin in 1932. Filled with passion and even erotic energy, they reflect the depth of her love for Forster. "I think of you much and dream of you every night," she writes him, "and if my dreams could affect you over long distance, I am sure they would keep you awake."[17]

Or this: "My desire for you is a painful rather than pleasurable emotion. It is a ravishing hunger which makes me want you more than anything in the world and makes me feel as though I could barely exist until I saw you again."[18]

Dorothy Day with Forster Batterham

When she felt compelled to become a Catholic and Forster refused to get married, she separated from him. In *The*

Long Loneliness she says it was literally a choice between God and man. But, as the letters demonstrate, the break was not nearly as clear-cut as that. For the next five years she desperately hoped and prayed that Forster would change his mind and consent to marry her. So deep was her attachment to him that she felt she had to flee New York—moving with her daughter Tamar to California, then to Mexico and to Florida—to resist the temptation to be with him. "Do I have to be condemned to celibacy all my days, just because of your pig-headedness?"[19]

The letters have an almost unbearable pathos: "The ache in my heart is intolerable at times, and sometimes for days I can feel your lips upon me, waking and sleeping. It is because I love you so much that I want you to marry me. I want to be in your arms every night, as I used to be, and be with you always."[20] But in the end she realized that this was not to be. On December 10, 1932 she wrote what would the last of her letters to Forster for many years. She spoke again of her deep love for him and her wish to marry. But in the end, she acknowledged, "It is all hopeless . . . I have really given up now, so I won't try to persuade you anymore."[21] Note that this was written two days after her visit to the Shrine of the Immaculate Conception, which offers a new context for appreciating a prayer "which came with tears and anguish" that she might discover her vocation. It was that same month that she found Peter Maurin waiting for her. It is as if one door closed while another opened on the rest of her life.

It is extraordinary to realize on the one hand how much her vocation depended on Forster's commitment to his own principles. If it had been up to Dorothy, she would have married Forster, raised a houseful of children, and continued writing novels and plays. There would have been no Catholic Worker.

At the same time, this story dramatizes the deep sacrifice that lay at the heart of Dorothy's vocation. It was the foundation for a lifetime of courage, perseverance, and dedication. It marked her deep sense of the heroic demands of faith. It also accounted for the high standards to which she held her friends and associates. Writing to a former *Catholic Worker* editor, after learning that he planned to remarry without seeking an annulment, she advised him to resign as secretary of a Catholic peace organization. "When God asks great things of us," she wrote, "great sacrifices, He intends to do great things with us; though they will seem small, they will be most important. Who knows the power of the Spirit? God's grace is more powerful than all the nuclear weapons that could possibly be accumulated."[22]

DOROTHY DAY WAS A WITNESS to or participant in many of the great social and ecclesial movements of her day. She traveled to Cuba after the Revolution. She fasted in Rome during Vatican II; she was shot at by the Ku Klux Klan in Georgia; she was arrested at the age of seventy-five while picketing in California with the United Farmworkers. But her diaries are a reminder that most of any life is occupied with ordinary activities and pursuits. Inspired by her favorite saint, Therese of Lisieux, Dorothy was convinced that ordinary life was actually the true arena for holiness. Her spirituality was focused on the effort to practice forgiveness, charity, and patience with those closest at hand.

Here the title of her diaries, *The Duty of Delight*, really summarizes her approach to life. She believed that delight, like love, is a matter of discipline, a matter of the will. It is one thing to feel delight when things are delightful. It is one thing to love people who are loveable. But the heart of the gospel is adding love, even where there is no love; loving the person beside us— even if that person is disagreeable. If you will to love someone, if you will to see Christ in that person, you can do it—this is what Dorothy believed. That didn't mean this was any easier for her than for the rest of us. But it was the exercise of charity in these small ways that equipped her for the extraordinary and heroic actions she performed on a wider stage.

Like most holy people, she often fell short of her ideals. We know this because she herself calls attention to her faults: her impatience, her capacity for anger and self-righteousness. "Thinking gloomily of the sins and shortcomings of others," she writes, "it suddenly came to me to remember my own offenses, just as heinous as those of others. If I concern myself with my own sins and lament them, if I remember my own failures and lapses, I will not be resentful of others. This was most cheering and lifted the load of gloom from my mind. It makes one unhappy to judge people and happy to love them."[23]

Someone once told Dorothy to "hold her temper," and she responded, "I hold more temper in one minute than you will in your entire life." In her diary she writes, "I have a hard enough job to curb the anger in my own heart which I sometimes even wake up with, go to sleep with—a giant to strive with, an ugliness, a sorrow to me—a mighty struggle to love. As long as there is any resentment, bitterness, lack of love in my own heart I am powerless. God must help me."[24]

The diaries offer a frank and candid picture of the strain and stress of Catholic Worker life: the overwhelming demands on Dorothy's time and attention, the rebukes and resentments she faced from those in her own community, the demands of leadership. "I fail people daily," she wrote. "God help me, when they come to me for aid and sympathy. There are too many of them, whichever way I turn. It is not that I can do anything. I must always disappoint them and arouse their bitterness, especially when it is material things they want. But I deny them the Christ in me when I do not show them tenderness, love. God forgive me, and make up to them for it."[25]

Often she refers to her temptation to simply walk away from the Catholic Worker: "The opposition to the work, the idea that I did not understand or interpret Peter Maurin correctly... There has been many an occasion when I never wanted to see a CW [Catholic Worker] again." But then, she adds: "Some such thought as that of St. John of the Cross would come, 'Where there is no love, put love, and you will find love,' and make all right. When it comes down to it, even on the natural plane, it is much happier and more enlivening to love than to be loved."[26]

She reacted strongly against the loose sexual mores of the 1960s counterculture, and she resisted their intrusion at the Worker. At the same time, the memory of her own youthful struggles made her particularly sensitive to the searching and sufferings of youth. To a young woman in distress she wrote, "Please forgive me for presuming to write you so personally—to intrude on you and your suffering, as I am doing, but I felt I had to—because I have gone thru so much the same suffering as you in the confusion of my youth and my search for love…It is a very real agony of our own, wanting human love, fulfillment, and one so easily sees all the imperfections of this love we seek, the inability of others ever to satisfy this need of ours, the constant failure of those nearest and dearest to understand, to respond."[27]

Dorothy Day toward the end of her earthly pilgrimage

In response to the insecurity, the sorrows, and drudgery of life among the "insulted and injured," she tried always to remember "the duty of delight": "I was thinking how, as one gets older, we are tempted to sadness, knowing life as it is here on earth, the suffering, the Cross. And how we must overcome it daily, growing in love, and the joy which goes with loving."[28]

And through her diaries and letters we see her gradually slowing down, adjusting, after a heart attack, to the end of her restless pilgrimage. She had traveled the world; she had spent much of her life on a constant bus trip from one end of the country to the other. First she was confined to the city, then to Maryhouse, and finally to her room on the second floor, where she spent much of her time gazing out the window at life outside on East Third Street, which the Catholic Worker shared with the Hells Angels. In her youth, she writes, she had received a great "revelation": that for anyone attuned to the life of the mind, the future held the promise of unending fascination. And now she could observe, "No matter how old I get…no matter how feeble, short of breath, incapable of walking more than a few blocks, what with heart murmurs, heart failure, emphysema perhaps, arthritis in feet and knees, with all these symptoms of age and decrepitude, my heart can still leap for joy as I read and suddenly assent to some great truth enunciated by some great mind and heart."[29]

That intense interest in life continued as she took in the world around her and rummaged increasingly in the "rag-bag" of memory. She had always been a "compulsive" writer, and writing was virtually the last thing to go. Toward the end, her newspaper columns reverted to short, breathless excerpts from her diary—just enough, she said, "to let people know I am still alive." She kept writing until a few days before her death on November 29, 1980.

Yes, she was old. And yet her sense of adventure, her idealism, her "instinct for the heroic" always connects her in my mind with the spirit of youth. Though she grew hard of hearing and bent with age, she never acquired the cynicism or spirit of compromise that is a proverbial mark of maturity. She was already seventy-five when she was arrested with the farmworkers, when she risked arrest by refusing to pay federal taxes, when she started a new house of hospitality for homeless women in New York City. Until the end she was surrounded by young people, and they have continued in large numbers to be drawn to her story and inspired to take up her mission.

I was back in college when I received word of her death. I remembered our last meeting in her room at Maryhouse that fall, surrounded by her favorite books, icons, and picture postcards. After five years at the Catholic Worker I had become a Catholic. "Well, now you'll have a better idea of what you're interested in," she said. She told me that my mother had once written to her, thanking her for all she had done for me. (I hadn't known this.) She embraced me with a maternal kiss. "Don't forget about us," she said. And then she remembered that I had told her I would be studying literature. "What about Dostoevsky?" she asked. "What's your favorite of his novels?"

I THINK ABOUT HER NOW, all these years later, in these times we are living through, when the gospel narrative is again dismissed as foolish and irrelevant in the face of terrorism, surveillance, and endless war. We see the growing chasm between rich and poor, so many hungry, so many in prison, so many in search of work; the struggle of immigrants to be treated with dignity, the contempt that is directed at the poor and unemployed as mere "takers"; the virtual criminalization of anyone with the "wrong" color skin. We see the earth ravaged in a short-term search for resources. We see our wasteful consumerism contributing to the perils of climate change, while nuclear weapons continue to hold humanity hostage.

Dorothy Day and Peter Maurin had answers for all these problems—answers they found plainly in the gospels. And once again they raise the question: What would our society look like if it were organized around values of compassion, justice, solidarity, and concern for the common good rather than selfishness, greed, and fear?

Many years ago I gave a talk on the centenary of Dorothy's birth and used the occasion to lay out the case for her canonization. I highlighted what I saw as her primary gifts to the church, including her inspiration to the lay apostolate, her initiative in combining the practice of charity with the struggle for justice, and her practice of gospel nonviolence. Dorothy did more than any Catholic in modern times to recall the peace witness of Jesus, and she lived to see so many of her principles vindicated in the teaching of the church.

Now that same church has taken up the cause for her canonization, a long, laborious process that may result one day in her being officially named St. Dorothy. Whatever opinion Dorothy might have had of such a process, you can be sure that she would have objected to any effort to airbrush her faults and failings, to put her on a pedestal and out of reach, to make her seem unapproachable, otherworldly, and mysterious.

I know that among Dorothy's admirers there are many who remain skeptical about the process of canonization. As Ken Woodward noted many years ago in his book *Making Saints*, whereas in most cases the question is whether a person is worthy of canonization, in the case of Dorothy Day the question is often whether the process of canonization is worthy of her. There are legitimate concerns about whether her message will be coopted or watered down or adapted to some agenda that was not her own. And yet Dorothy had great respect for the ways of the church. Those who feel she is too good for its corrupt machinations may be the ones who are putting her on a pedestal she would have disdained.

The fact is, if there is real thought about her canonization today, this is in large part a reflection of how far the church has traveled in catching up with her witness. Particularly in the context of the era of Pope Francis, one can imagine that the cause for Dorothy Day's canonization may contribute to the ongoing program of renewal of the church. The benefits that may come from her canonization belong to the church of the future—not just the church as it will be in generations to come, but the church as it might be.

In the purity of her vision and in her courageous witness she continues to walk ahead, beckoning the church to follow. It falls on those who honor her humanity to tell her story without softening any of her radical edges.

At the end of the day, the fundamental significance of Dorothy's "cause" rests not just in her own example of holiness but in the way she held up the vocation of holiness as the common calling of all Christians. She did not believe holiness was just for a few—or for those dedicated to formal religious life. It was simply a matter of taking seriously the logic of our baptismal vows—to put off the old person and put on Christ; to grow constantly in our capacity for love.

She lived out her own vocation in the Catholic Worker movement. But she set an example for all Christians, especially lay people, reminding us that the gospel is meant to be lived, and challenging us to find our own unique path of faithful discipleship.

Dorothy Day was a great believer in what Jean-Pierre de Caussade called "the sacrament of the present moment." In each situation, in each encounter, in each task before us, she believed, there is a path to God. We don't need to be in a monastery or a chapel. We don't need to become a different person first. We can start today, this moment, where we are, to add to the balance of love in the world, to add to the balance of peace.

4

Thomas Merton
Spiritual Explorer

"In one sense we are always traveling, and traveling as
if we did not know where we were going.
In another sense we have already arrived."
—*The Seven Storey Mountain*

In 1968, as Thomas Merton embarked on his final journey to
Asia, he wrote in his journal, "May I not come back without having settled the great affair. And found also the great compassion
. . . I am going home, to the home where I have never been in this
body."[1]

Merton had spent his early life on a grand tour that took
him—as he summarized in the final paragraph of *The Seven
Storey Mountain*—"from Prades to Bermuda to St. Antonin to
Oakham to London to Cambridge to Rome to New York to Columbia to Corpus Christi to St. Bonaventure to the Cistercian
Abbey of the poor men who labor in Gethsemani." To what end?
He answered that implicit question in the voice of God: "That
you may become the brother of God and learn to know the Christ
of the burnt men."[2]

He would remain at the Abbey of Gethsemani for the last
twenty-seven years of his life, but that was certainly not the end

Portions of this chapter were first published as "On Spiritual Explo-
ration," in, *What I Am Living For: Lessons from the Life and Writings
of Thomas Merton*, ed. Jon M. Sweeney (Notre Dame, IN: Ave Maria,
2018), 29–42.

point of a journey, now more interior than geographical. He acknowledged as much in the Latin motto that concluded his autobiography, *Sit finis libri, non finis quarendi*: "Here ends the book, but not the searching." Truer words were never spoken.

In fact, Merton's life continued to be marked by a restless search that would last until his death. In his struggle to plunge deeper into the divine mystery and the depths of his own vocation, he traveled onward toward his true home—the home where he had never been in this body.

MERTON FIRST CAME to the attention of the world in 1948 through the publication of *The Seven Storey Mountain,* an autobiography, written under obedience, during his early years as a Trappist monk. It told a story—by turns funny and sad—of his search for his true identity and home. His parents were artists— an American mother and a father from New Zealand—who met in France, where Thomas was born. His mother died when he was six; his father ten years later. Thomas spent his early life moving between France, Long Island, Bermuda, and England. By his own account, his early life was marked by careless, if not reckless, self-indulgence—sufficiently scandalous to cause his guardian to send him packing from Cambridge University back to New York, where he completed his studies at Columbia University. There he quickly became a big man on campus, perfecting a pose of cool sophistication, smoking, drinking all night in jazz clubs, and writing novels in the style of James Joyce. He regarded himself as a true man of his age, free of any moral laws beyond those of his own making, ready to "ransack and rob the world of all its pleasures and satisfactions." But increasingly his life struck him more as a story of pride and selfishness that brought nothing but unhappiness to himself and others. "What a strange thing!" he wrote, "In filling myself, I had emptied myself. In grasping things, I had lost everything. In devouring pleasures and joys, I had found distress and anguish and fear."[3]

Out of this anguish and confusion, Merton found himself drawn by the sense that there must be a deeper end and purpose to existence. All around him the world was tumbling toward war, the ultimate achievement of "contemporary civilization." Meanwhile he was reading Blake, St. Augustine, and medieval philosophy and beginning to suspect that "the only way to live was in a world that was charged with the presence and reality of God."[4]

It was a short leap from this insight to his decision to become a Catholic. He found in the gospel some answer to the deep questions in his life: a certain healing, some kind of order, and rule for living. He was baptized at the Church of Corpus Christi near the Columbia campus. But for Merton, his conversion to Catholicism was only the beginning of a deeper spiritual quest—a call that required a total response.

In his memoir he describes how one of his college friends asked him what he wanted to be now that he was a Catholic. "I don't know," he said. "I guess what I want is to be a good Catholic."

"What you should say," his friend corrected him, "is that you want to be a saint... The secret to be a saint is to want to be one. Don't you believe that God will make you what He created you to be, if you will consent to let Him do it?"[5]

Much of Merton's subsequent journey could be seen as a response to that challenge, the challenge to go all the way, to be what God had created him to be—in the context of a continuously evolving understanding of what that really meant.

Quite soon Merton came to believe it was not enough for him simply to teach English at a Franciscan college, or even to work in the slums of Harlem. God was calling for a greater sacrifice: nothing less than everything. He considered becoming a priest and made some steps toward entering the Franciscans. But his heart was won when he read an article in *The Catholic Encyclopedia* about the Trappists. Officially known as the Cistercians of the Strict Observance, the Trappists were a seventeenth-century reform branch of the Cistercian Order, itself a twelfth-century reform movement within the Benedictine monastic tradition extending back to the sixth century. The Trappists sought to restore the austere discipline of early monasticism, with a greater emphasis on manual labor, regular prayer, and a strict spirit of silence.

This was the order Merton encountered in the pages of *The Catholic Encyclopedia*. As he wrote, what he read "pierced me to the heart like a knife...What wonderful happiness there was, then, in the world! There were still men on this miserably noisy, cruel earth, who tasted the marvelous joy of silence and solitude, who dwelt in forgotten mountain cells, in secluded monasteries, where the news and desires and appetites and conflicts of the world no longer reached them...The thought of those monasteries, those remote choirs, those cells, those hermitages, those cloisters, those men in their cowls, the poor monks, the men who had become nothing, shattered my heart. In an instant the desire of those solitudes was wide open within me, like a wound."[6]

It was of course a completely romantic response. At this point he had not actually met a single example of these happy monks. Yet when he eventually went on a retreat at the Abbey of Gethsemani, the Trappist monastery near Bardstown, Kentucky, the experience totally lived up to his expectations. He felt he had found his true home at last. "This is the center of America," he wrote. "It is an axle around which the whole country blindly turns...This is the cause and reason why the nation is holding together."[7]

When he returned to the secular world, everything seemed to him "insipid and slightly insane." The world was again tumbling into war—an image of hell, as Merton saw it, that was also an image writ large of his own ego, greed, and selfishness. He returned to Gethsemani and was admitted as a novice on December 10, 1941, just days after Pearl Harbor. He sought a life of prayer and penance; he desired to "give everything." And so, as he writes, "Brother Matthew locked the gate behind me and I was enclosed in the four walls of my new freedom."[8]

In entering the monastery Merton not only felt he was leaving the world and giving up "everything"; he was also leaving behind a certain "Thomas Merton," with all his anxious desire to "be somebody," his demanding ego, his tendency to sarcasm and scorn for people who didn't meet his standards. With the anonymous monks in their white habits, he intended to drown to the world, to be invisible, a nobody.

It didn't quite go that way.

Ordination of Thomas Merton, Abbey of Gethsemani, May 26, 1949

The Seven Storey Mountain turned into an astonishing success, selling six hundred thousand copies in cloth in the first year. Merton was suddenly the most famous monk in America. The irony was not lost on him. And yet his superiors felt his writing had something to offer the world and they ordered him to keep at it. And so he did. There followed books of poetry, lives of Trappist saints (which he later deemed "awful"), books on monasticism, and an ongoing stream of books on prayer and the spiritual life. If he ever doubted whether he was a true monk, there was never any doubt that he was truly a writer.

Yet for all the books he would go on to produce, in the public mind he was eternally fixed at the point where his memoir had ended—as a young monk with his cowl pulled over his head, happily convinced that in joining an austere medieval community he had fled the modern world, never to return. It was difficult for readers to appreciate that this picture represented only the beginning of Merton's journey as a monk.

One aspect of the book that he particularly came to regret was the attitude of pious scorn directed at "the world" and its unfortunate denizens. He had seemed to regard the monastery as a secluded haven set apart from "the news and desires and appetites and conflicts" that bedeviled ordinary humanity.

In 1948 an errand in Louisville occasioned one of his first trips outside the monastery. In his journal, he noted piously, "Going into Louisville the other day, I wasn't struck by anything in particular. Although I felt completely alienated from everything in the world and all its activity." While he felt the people were "worthy of sympathizing with," overall, he judged the excursion "boring."[9]

What a difference a decade would make! Ten years later, in 1958, he records in his journals the radically different impact of another errand in Louisville. "On the corner of Fourth and Walnut in the center of the shopping district"—an intersection that has been rechristened Thomas Merton Plaza—he experienced a moment of mystical awareness that inspired one of the most famous passages in all his books. He writes:

> I was suddenly overwhelmed with the realization that I loved all those people, that they were mine and I theirs, that we could not be alien to one another even though we were total strangers. It was like waking from a dream of separateness, of spurious self-isolation in a special world, the world of renunciation and supposed holiness.
>
> The whole illusion of a separate holy existence is a dream. Not that I question the reality of my vocation, or of my monastic life; but the conception of "separation from the world" that we have in the monastery too easily presents itself as a complete illusion: the illusion that by making vows we become a different species of being, pseudo-angels, spiritual men, men of interior life, what have you.[10]

The passage ends with the words, "There is no way of telling people that they are all walking around shining like the sun ... There are no strangers! ... The gate of heaven is everywhere."

It is worth underlining these words: "*It was like waking from a dream of separateness, of spurious self-isolation in a special world, the world of renunciation and supposed holiness.*" In that dream of separateness he is describing an understanding of holiness that had animated his early life as a monk. It is an understanding of holiness primarily defined by ascetical self-denial. In its place would come an understanding of holiness based on compassionate solidarity with his fellow human beings. And so Merton came to see that the entire purpose of the monastic life, or any spiritual search for that matter, is to achieve this vision, this awakening from a dream of separateness, to realize our underlying oneness, our unity in what he called "a hidden wholeness."

No doubt this marked a crucial turning point in his evolution as a monk. For years Merton had devoted creative thought to the meaning of monastic and contemplative life. But from this point on he became increasingly concerned with making connections between the monastery and the wider world. His writing assumed a more ecumenical and compassionate tone. Reading his old writing, he observes, "I cannot go back to the earlier fervor or the asceticism that accompanied it. The new fervor will be rooted not in asceticism but in humanism." For Merton it was a kind of rebirth. "I am finally coming out of the chrysalis," he writes. "Now [I face] the pain and struggle of fighting my way out into something new and much bigger. I must see and embrace God in the whole world."[11]

This increasing openness was also reflected in his writings on holiness. Previously, in thrall to a dream of separateness and "supposed holiness," he had held up the monastery as an ideal arena for achieving sanctity. Now he wrote that being a saint was simply a matter of consenting to God's creative love. "The pale flowers of the dogwood outside this window are saints," he wrote. "The lakes hidden among the hills are saints, and the sea too is a saint who praises God without interruption in her majestic dance."[12]

And what about human beings, for whom the problem of sanctity is a little more complicated? "For me sanctity consists in being myself," he wrote. "For me to be saint means to be myself. Therefore the problem of sanctity and salvation is in fact the problem of finding out who I am and of discovering my true self."

Another way of putting this would be in terms of abandoning the false self, the mask we present to the world and to ourselves.

The whole journey of Thomas Merton to this point could be seen as putting off a series of masks—the bad boy, the sophisticated twentieth-century man, the good Catholic, the perfect monk—to become his true self, the saint, as his Columbia friend had put it, that God created him to be. But it was the same challenge for everyone. The path to sanctity for Thomas Merton the monk was not really so very different from the path of every other person in the world.

Suddenly Merton began reaching out to an ever-widening circle of correspondents, including the Russian novelist Boris Pasternak, the Polish intellectual Czeslaw Milosz, the Zen master D. T. Suzuki, the Beat poet Lawrence Ferlinghetti, feminist theologian Rosemary Ruether, Rabbi Abraham Heschel, and Dorothy Day, founder of the pacifist Catholic Worker movement in New York City. Writing to Dorothy Day, he offered wholehearted support for her brave acts of civil disobedience against compulsory civil defense drills in New York—agreeing with her that these drills were really rehearsals for doomsday. As for his own writing, he noted in a letter to her, "I don't feel that I can in conscience, at a time like this, go on writing just about things like meditation...I cannot just bury my head in a lot of rather tiny and secondary monastic studies either. I think I have to face the big issues, the life and death issues: and this is what everyone is afraid of."[13]

Along with his writings on prayer and spirituality he began to write prophetic essays on the "big issues," particularly the Cold War atmosphere of fear and the threat of nuclear war—many of these articles published in the *Catholic Worker*. In the first of these, he wrote, "Peace is to be preached, nonviolence is to be explained as a practical method, and not left to be mocked as an outlet for crackpots, who want to make a show of themselves... It is the great Christian task of our time. Everything else is secondary, for the survival of the human race depends on it." The sober preparation for nuclear war, he believed, was the surest sign that we were "no longer living in a Christian world." The logic of events was guiding us toward an unimaginable crime, the possibility of "global suicide," the free choice of which, "would be moral evil second only to the crucifixion."[14]

In reflections on the mentality of Adolf Eichmann, one of the architects of the Holocaust, Merton was struck by the determination of psychiatrists who examined him that Eichmann was totally sane. Applying that standard to the work of nuclear war planners, Merton considered that we were living in a time when perfectly sane men, following the dictates of reason and logic, were capable of engineering the destruction of the earth. In such a time, what was needed were men and women of imagination—poets, rebels, prophets, and yes, monks—who could pierce the shell of functional logic to act on the basis of a deeper spiritual wisdom and share that vision with others.

The social crises that Merton addressed, he believed, were, ultimately spiritual issues. They were rooted in a distorted spiritual vision in which we failed to recognize our underlying oneness. This was the vision that underlay his mystical epiphany at Fourth and Walnut. Referring to the people he saw on the street, he had written, "If only they could all see themselves as they really *are*. If only we could see each other that way all the time. There would be no more war, no more hatred, no more cruelty, no more greed..."[15]

Not everyone, to be sure, was happy with this new Thomas Merton. They preferred "the official voice of Trappist silence, the monk with his hood up and his back to the camera, brooding over the waters of an artificial lake." The new Merton, he wrote, "was not the petulant and uncanonizable modern Jerome who never got over the fact that he could give up beer." To this, he added words intended to shock his pious devotees: "I drink beer whenever I can lay my hands on any. I love beer, and by that very act, the world."[16] As for his famous memoir, he had reached the point of stating, with some exasperation, "*The Seven Storey Mountain* is the work of a man I never even heard of."[17]

Among those who were especially unhappy were the censors of the Trappist order, who ordered him to cease publication on topics of war and peace. He resorted for a time to circulating his writings in mimeographed form, until the publication of Pope John XXIII's encyclical *Pacem in Terris* signaled that the coast was clear. The censorship was lifted and he resumed his writings on topical issues, including the struggle against racism and what he called "the overwhelming atrocity" of the Vietnam War. He believed his love for the world implied a prophetic stance, a need to criticize its spiritual delusions and to struggle, in collaboration with like-minded spiritual seekers, "to make the world better, more free, more just, more livable, more human." In a preface to the Japanese edition of the *Seven Storey Mountain* he put it more specifically:

> It is my intention to make my entire life a rejection of, a protest against the crimes and injustices of war and political tyranny which threaten to destroy the whole race of man and world with him. By my monastic life and vows I am saying NO to all the concentration camps, the aerial bombardments, the staged political trials, the judicial murders, the racial injustices, the economic tyrannies, and the whole socio-economic apparatus which seems geared for nothing but global destruction...If I say NO to all these secular forces, I also say YES to all that is good in the world and in man. I say YES to all that is beautiful in nature...[18]

While many of Merton's readers wished he would stick with the old writing on the liturgy and prayer, there were also new friends who wondered what he was doing holed up in a monastery; wasn't this life of prayer and solitude a cop-out from the more relevant action in the streets? For Merton, this never posed a serious temptation. In fact, his increasing engagement with the world outside the monastery was accompanied by a deeper call to solitude.

MONKS IN THE BENEDICTINE TRADITION, including Trappists like Merton, take a vow of what is called "stability." In a literal sense, this is a vow to remain in the monastery to which they are attached. It is a commitment not to run away when things get tough, or to imagine that life will be easier if you just don't have to put up with all the idiots around you. What you find disturbing has its roots inside; if you leave, you will just take it with you somewhere else. But there is a deeper principle involved than just staying put. Complementing the vow of stability is a second Benedictine principle called *"conversatio morum"*—literally, the conversion of manners. Essentially it refers to the ongoing process of growth and spiritual maturity, going deeper into the heart of your vocation. The task of becoming a monk doesn't end when you take your vows; it is an ongoing journey that lasts a lifetime.

There is no doubt that for Thomas Merton the vow of stability was a particular challenge. In his early book *The Sign of Jonas*, he described stability as the belly of the whale, the mysterious paradox through which, like the prophet Jonah, he was being carried to his ultimate destination.

Though his early monastic writings describe a feeling of giddy homecoming, his later journals tell a different story: irritation with the banal business operations of the monastery; conflicts with his abbot; frustration with a religious system that seems determined to stifle his yearnings for a life of solitary prayer.

In his early years he was beset by the notion of joining a "purer" order, the Carthusians or the Camaldolese. This later gave way to fantasies of fleeing to a hermitage or a community in Mexico, Nicaragua, Chile, the Virgin Islands, New Mexico, or

Alaska—seemingly anywhere but Gethsemani. Inevitably these plans were quashed by his superiors, if they had not already been replaced by newer schemes. In light of such frustrations he could write, "I think the monastic life as we live it here warps people. Kills their spirit, reduces them to something less than human."[19] He proclaims to his journal, "It is intolerable to have to spend my life contributing to the maintenance of this illusion. The illusion of the great, gay, joyous, peppy, optimistic, Jesus-loving, one hundred percent American Trappist monastery."[20] (At the time when he wrote this, Merton was the novice master for the monastery!)

Eventually, Merton realized that he didn't need to leave Gethsemani; what he really wanted was greater interior space to define the meaning of his contemplative vocation. It was a call not to leave the monastery but to rediscover its inner meaning. "It does not much matter where you are, as long as you can be at peace about it and live your life. The place certainly will not live my life for me. I have to live it for myself."[21]

Where would he find the solitude he sought? "Here or there makes no difference. Somewhere, nowhere, beyond all 'where.' Solitude outside geography, or in it. No matter."[22]

At this point, after years of clamoring for a more solitary life, Merton was given permission to live in a simple hermitage on the monastery grounds, a situation that proved conducive both to prayer and creative work. Happily, he wrote of "the sense of a journey ended, of wandering at an end. The first time in my life I ever really felt that I had come home and that my roaming and looking were ended."[23]

In the pure silence and solitude of his hermitage, Merton felt he was making his own kind of protest against a world in which communication had been replaced by party platforms and advertising slogans; in which time and existence itself were measured out and weighed for their productive value. In an ironic piece, "A Signed Confession of Crimes against the State," he wrote, "My very existence is an admission of guilt ... The very thoughts of a person like me are crimes against the state. All

I have to do is think and immediately I become guilty." Going on, he added, "I confess that I am sitting under a pine tree doing absolutely nothing. I have done nothing for one hour and firmly intend to do nothing for an indefinite pe-

Thomas Merton's hermitage

riod. I have taken my shoes off. I confess that I have been listening to a mockingbird. Yes, I admit that it is a mockingbird... This kind of thing goes on all the time. Wherever I am, I find myself the center of reactionary plots like this one."[24]

As a spiritual explorer, he felt a special connection with the Desert Fathers of the fourth century, who had left the comforts and compromises of a supposedly Christian world for the solitude of the wilderness. In words that really applied to himself, he wrote, "What the [Desert] Fathers sought most of all was their own true self, in Christ. And in order to do this, they had to reject completely the false, formal self, fabricated under social compulsion in 'the world.' They sought a way to God that was uncharted and freely chosen, not inherited from others who had mapped it out beforehand... We need to learn from these men of the fourth century how to ignore prejudice, defy compulsion and strike out fearlessly into the unknown."[25]

Merton himself, of course, was seeking a "way to God that was uncharted and freely chosen, not inherited from others who had mapped it out beforehand." Unfortunately, there are risks to be faced by those who travel without maps. The solitary desert explorers whom Merton admired faced many such perils in the form of temptations. The same was true for Merton. It was soon after settling into his hermitage that he faced his own final and most difficult temptation: falling in love and conducting a secret affair with a young nurse whom he had met in the hospital in Louisville.

This episode, which lasted over a period of several months, is described in great detail in volume 6 of his published journals. The story is too complex to summarize adequately. Suffice to say that in this affair Merton experienced a liberating sense of his capacity to love and receive love. His journal is by turns deeply moving, heartbreaking, and also exasperating. Some have romanticized the episode, feeling that he should have—as one of his poet friends put it—"follow[ed] the ecstasy," right out of the monastery. That was a serious option. But what was not an option was to have it both ways—to suppose that there was some way to be both a hermit and a lover. What was at stake was not simply the violation of his monastic vows, but a kind of doubleness and lack of integrity. "What do I fear most? Forgetting and ignorance of the inmost truth of my being. To forget who I am, to be lost in what I am not, to fail my own inner truth, to get carried away in what is not true to me..."[26]

When he was honest with himself he realized that he was ultimately wedded to his vocation to solitude. Regarding his vows, he wrote, "I cannot be true to myself if I am not true to so deep a commitment."[27] He came to the conclusion that his vocation was not just for himself, but that it meant something to the rest of the world.

> Vocation is more than just a matter of being in a certain place and wearing a certain kind of costume. There are too many people in the world who rely on the fact that I am serious about deepening an inner dimension of experience that they desire that is closed to them. And it is not closed to me. This is a gift that has been given me not for myself but for everyone...I cannot let it be squandered and dissipated foolishly. It would be criminal to do so.[28]

In effect he returned to the idea that had first attracted him to the Abbey—that the monastery was in some sense the *axis mundi*, that the monks were in some way, with their prayers and their faithfulness, keeping the world turning. But now he was understanding faithfulness not just in terms of an outward form or a particular setting, but in terms of the deepest core of himself. The difference suggested that this was not some special vocation for Trappist monks. Wherever people did this, wherever they were faithful to their true selves, they were the *axis mundi:* in standing up for peace and against lies, in the integrity of their witness, in creating something beautiful and true, in their loving service of their neighbors...For some this might be in a soup kitchen, a studio, a marriage, or a prison cell. For him, it was in his hermitage.

On September 10, 1966 he signed a short formula in which he committed himself "to live in solitude for the rest of my life." Nevertheless, he continued to be carried toward his true destiny in the belly of a paradox, traveling without maps, stumbling in the dark, but trusting that he was being guided toward his true home.

IN 1968, THE LAST YEAR OF HIS LIFE, a more flexible abbot permitted him at last to venture forth. He made several short, unpublicized trips before accepting an invitation to address an international conference of Christian monks in Bangkok. Merton was particularly excited about the prospect of exploring his deep interest in Eastern spirituality. In this respect, as his journals show, the trip marked a new breakthrough, another wider encounter with the "gate of heaven" that is everywhere. He met with Buddhist and Hindu monks. In India he had several significant meetings with the Dalai Lama.

He concluded an address to an interfaith gathering in Calcutta with these words: "The deepest level of communication is not communication, but communion. It is wordless. It is beyond words and it is beyond speech, and it is beyond concept. Not that we discover a new unity. We discover an older unity. My dear brothers, we are already one. But we imagine that we are not. And what we have to recover is our original unity. What we have to be is what we are."[29]

In Ceylon, one week before his death, in the presence of the enormous statues of the reclining (dying) Buddha in Polonnaruwa, he was "suddenly, almost forcibly, jerked clean out of the habitual, half-tied vision of things, and an inner clearness, clarity, as if exploding from the rocks themselves, became evident and obvious...everything is emptiness and everything is compassion." It was the culmination of his Asian pilgrimage: "I mean, I know and have seen what I was obscurely looking for."[30] And perhaps it was something more.

On December 10 he delivered his talk in Bangkok before retiring to his room for a shower and a nap. In this talk, in the last hour of his life, he spoke, significantly, of the monastic principle of *conversatio morum,* calling it the most mysterious and yet most essential of all monastic vows. He interpreted it as "a commitment to total inner transformation of one sort or another—a commitment to become a completely new man. It seems to me

Statues of the reclining Buddha in Polonnaruwa, Sri Lanka:
"Everything is emptiness and everything is compassion..."

that that could be regarded as the end of the monastic life, and that no matter where one attempts to do this, that remains the essential thing."[31]

A short while after delivering this talk he was found dead in his room, apparently electrocuted by the faulty wiring of a fan. His death on December 10, 1968, fell on the exact anniversary of his entry into Gethsemani in 1941, which in turn happened to be the exact halfway mark of his life; having entered the abbey at the age of twenty-seven, he died one month shy of his fifty-fourth birthday.

In Merton's writings there are many foreshadowings of this end. In his early journal, *The Sign of Jonas,* he concludes with a tour of the monastery during a nighttime "fire watch," ending in the belfry, where he imagines his hand on the door "through which I see the heavens. The door swings out upon a vast sea of darkness and of prayer. Will it come like this, the moment of my death? Will You open a door upon the great forest and set my feet upon a ladder under the moon, and take me out among the stars?"[32]

Likewise, he had concluded *The Seven Storey Mountain* with a mysterious speech in the voice of God, in which he contemplated his end:

> Do not ask when it will be or where it will be or how it will be: on a mountain, or in a prison, in a desert or in a concentration camp, or in a hospital or at Gethsemani. It does not matter. So do not ask me, because I am not going to tell you. You will not know until you are in it . . . But you shall taste the true solitude of my anguish and my poverty, and I shall lead you into the high places of my joy and you shall die in Me and find all things in My mercy which has created you for this end.[33]

During his life Merton published nearly fifty books, ranging from histories of monasticism, books on prayer and the spiritual life, several volumes of poetry, collections of essays covering such topics as Zen Buddhism and Eastern religion, Gandhi's philosophy of nonviolence, Native American spirituality, the novels of

Camus and Faulkner, and prophetic responses—still remarkably topical—to the problems of war, racism, and the desecration of nature. Posthumously, these books have been joined by nearly as many published works, including five volumes of his correspondence, collections of photographs and calligraphic art, and seven volumes of journals.

Apart from his brilliance as a writer, what accounts for the enduring interest in Merton? He was a poet and an artist, a born rebel who spent most of his life under a vow of obedience; a man thoroughly formed by the tempestuous currents of the twentieth century who found peace and meaning in an austere brand of monasticism rooted in the twelfth century; a Catholic priest who entered into creative dialogue with people of all faiths, especially the religions of the East; a man whose solitude became a watchtower, allowing him to discern with uncommon insight the pathologies of our time: the self-destructive materialism that leaves us spiritually impoverished; the mythology that divides humanity into opposing blocs that threaten global destruction. He was a man of the widest vision who wished to reach beyond the confines of his solitary life to enter into dialogue with writers, artists, activists, and visionaries of all traditions.

He was all these things, but for many who have been fascinated and inspired by his work, Merton is the consummate spiritual explorer—one who never ceased in the quest to know God and to know himself, to grow in the direction of a truth beyond words and images, and to report back on what he had discovered. For spiritual explorers like Merton, their message is ultimately rooted in their own inner journey. And for many spiritual seekers of the past fifty years, an encounter with Thomas Merton has been a significant milestone on their own journey.

That was certainly true for me. I discovered Merton when I was in high school, thanks to a family friend who grew tired of my pronouncements on the spiritual vacuity of the West. She gave me a copy of *Mystics and Zen Masters*. From Merton I discovered, among other things, that there was room in Christianity for engagement with Gandhi, Zen Buddhism, opposition to the war in Vietnam, and a general spirit of mischief that appealed to my teenaged sensibility. But it was much later, when I was at the Catholic Worker, that I discovered *The Seven Storey Mountain*, *New Seeds of Contemplation*, *Raids on the Unspeakable*, and other books that opened my heart to the world of silence. Soon after I had more or less decided to become a Catholic, I made a retreat at Gethsemani and experienced something of the allure that Merton had felt at a similar age. In the middle of the night, from the balcony of the guest house, overlooking the chapel choir of chanting brothers in their white cowls, I imagined what it would be like to "drown to the world," to become one of these "poor monks, the men who had become nothing," who were keeping the world turning with their prayers.

At night we were advised to go to sleep on a verse from scripture. I randomly flipped open the Bible and let my finger fall on a page from the New Testament. There I landed on Peter's words to Christ on Mount Tabor: "Lord, it is good for us to be here." That seemed auspicious. But it was positively uncanny, the next night, when my finger fell on the same verse in a *different* gospel! What did that mean? That it was good to remain in Gethsemani? To become a Catholic? To be *here* in some general Zen sense—wherever *here* might happen to be?

The spell of the monastery did not last. But Merton's influence did last. As the years and decades passed, the number of his books in my library grew to require their own large bookcase. Eventually these included anthologies, biographies, and two of his originally mimeographed manuscripts that I published at Orbis Books. And as I grew older, his books would not leave me alone. I would return and reread them from differing vantage points along my own spiritual journey. Sometimes it was his prophetic writings on peace, or his reflections on prayer, his dialogue with other religious paths, or the mercilessly honest self-examination in his journals that especially spoke to me. (Having always thought of him as a venerable elder, it came as a shock, on the fiftieth anniversary of his death, to realize that I had outlived him by ten years.) And one of the things he especially taught me was about the meaning of holiness—that the point of it all is not to try become another Thomas Merton or any other saint, but to become *my own true self.*

SO WHAT ARE THE ODDS that Thomas Merton himself might be canonized and named an official saint? Probably slim. Some years ago, in fact, the U.S. bishops took pains to remove his name from a proposed list of exemplary American Catholics to be included in a national catechism for young adults. Ostensibly, this was based on their doubt that young people today know much about him (with the implication that the less they know the better!). Secondarily, according to then-Bishop Wuerl, there was the concern that "we don't know all the details of the searching at the end of his life." How ironic: *sic finis libri; non finis quarendi* indeed! More than fifty years after his death, his search continues, with no end to the questions about his searching. It is hard to pin him down; he remains a moving target. As he wrote in his journal, "My ideas are always changing, always moving around one center, always seeing the center from somewhere else. I will always be accused of inconsistencies. I will no longer be there to hear the accusations."[34]

In fact, probably Merton would not wish to be included in a list of exemplary Catholics, or held up as a model of anything—whether hermit, writer, or bongo player. His greatest desire was always to be a man on the margins—in solidarity with all those others on the margins: the rebels and prophets, the outliers and misfits, the solitary explorers.

The church prefers its saints to fit into a more conventional mold. Merton, for all his obedient submission to authority over many years, still makes some people nervous. Though totally rooted in his Catholic faith and his priesthood, Merton seemed always straining to burst through neat, official boundaries, resisting efforts to pin him down, box him in, or use him as a poster boy for any cause or institution. Maybe this makes sense. As Merton himself wrote, perhaps with a dose of self-justification: "One of the first signs of a saint may well be the fact that other people do not know what to make of him. In fact they are not sure whether he is crazy or only proud...He cannot seem to make his life fit in with the books."[35]

And yet in his address to the U.S. Congress in 2015 Pope Francis cited Thomas Merton among the four "great Americans" (including Abraham Lincoln, Martin Luther King Jr., and Dorothy Day) whose "dreams" formed the basis of his speech. Of Merton, he said, "He remains a source of spiritual inspiration and a guide for many people." Notably, the pope singled out for special attention exactly the aspects of Merton's life that caused the most controversy in his life and apparently after his death: "Merton was above all a man of prayer, a thinker who challenged the certitudes of his time and opened new horizons for souls and for the Church. He was also a man of dialogue, a promoter of peace between peoples and religions."[36] Those familiar with the thinking of Pope Francis know that "certitude" is not a positive word in his vocabulary. As he has said, "Our life is not given to us like an opera libretto, in which all is written down; but it means going, walking, doing, searching, seeing...We must enter into the adventure of the quest for meeting God; we must let God search and encounter us...God is encountered walking along the path..."[37]

In that sense, perhaps, Merton represents a type of holiness particularly suited and necessary to our times. He let go of his possessions, his ego, his certainty, and even a spurious kind of "supposed holiness"—until he came to rest in God's emptiness and compassion.

God is encountered walking along the path... And as Merton showed, sometimes we walk that path without maps. Merton, the spiritual explorer, created his path by walking it. But in in his own struggle to be faithful, he created possibilities for many others to live with greater compassion, courage, and integrity. And through his writings he cast seeds of contemplation and communion that continue to bear fruit in diverse and unexpected places. For those of us who struggle to see the road before us, he is a welcome guide and companion.

5

Henri Nouwen
Restless Searcher

Standing before a blackboard in a crowded lecture hall at Yale Divinity School, where he had become one of the most popular professors, Henri Nouwen wrote the date of his birth, 1932. This was followed by a short line to another date, 2010,

Henri Nouwen teaching at Yale Divinity School

which was followed by a question mark. "This could represent my life," he told the audience, "a finite period with a beginning and an end." (Neither he nor his students could guess how much shorter the actual line would be.) Then he shook his head, drawing a new line from one end of the blackboard all the way across

---

This chapter draws on material delivered in a lecture at Yale Divinity School for a conference on Henri Nouwen and Thomas Merton on November 4, 2017, as well as material from my book, *The Saints' Guide to Happiness* (New York: Image Books, 2003).

to the other. "I have come from somewhere," he said, "and I am going someplace else."[1]

Nouwen was not a monk—though part of him wanted to be. Probably, St. Benedict would have included him among what he called, derisively, the "gyratory monks"—who restlessly "wander in different countries staying in various monasteries for three or four days at a time." Nevertheless, like his hero Thomas Merton, Nouwen appreciated the meaning of *conversatio morum*—which Merton called the most necessary of monastic vows: the ongoing struggle to go more deeply into the heart of one's vocation.

Like Merton, Nouwen was a spiritual explorer who invited readers to accompany him on his journey. Where that was ultimately leading him, he was not sure. Through his doubts, sufferings, and restless searching, he clung in faith to the confidence that our origins and our destination are hidden in the mystery of God. That being so, our task in this life—whether it is long or short, whether heavy with sorrows, light with blessings, or a combination of the two—is to find the path that conveys us toward that goal. Whether Henri found the home he was seeking is something he alone knows. But in his prolific writings, he left a trail for fellow seekers.

HENRI NOUWEN WAS BORN in the Netherlands on January 24, 1932. He was the eldest of four children. His father was a distinguished tax lawyer. Henri was particularly close to his warm and loving mother. At a very young age he felt called to the priesthood, and he was ordained in 1957. In 1964 he traveled to the United States to study psychology and spiritual direction and stayed on to teach at a number of distinguished schools— Notre Dame, Yale Divinity School, and Harvard Divinity School. By the time of his passing, thirty-two years later in 1996, he had become one of the most popular and influential spiritual writers in the world. His popularity was only enhanced by his willingness to share his own struggles and brokenness.

He did not present himself as a "spiritual master," but—like the title of one of his early books—a "wounded healer." Those who knew him were aware of how deep his wounds ran. He was afflicted by an inordinate need for affection and affirmation; he was beset by anxieties about his identity and self-worth; there seemed to be a void within that could not be filled.

Nouwen had a great gift for friendship, and wherever he went he sowed the seeds of community. But still something drove him from one place or project to another. This included the sabbatical he spent as a "guest monk" at the Trappist Abbey of the Genesee in New York—an experience he described in his breakthrough book, *Genesee Diary.*

Undoubtedly, he was drawn there in part by his early attraction to Merton—the subject of one of his very first books. They had met one time at Gethsemani—though it seems that Merton, possibly having trouble with Henri's accent, didn't really get his name. He refers in his journals to a pleasant talk with a "Fr. Nau" from Holland. Nouwen shared a bit of Merton's restless nature, as he indicated in his introduction to the *Genesee Diary.* "My desire to live for seven months in a Trappist Monastery, not as a guest but as a monk, did not develop overnight. It was the outcome of many years of restless searching...I kept stumbling over my own compulsions and illusions. What was driving me from one book to another, one place to another, one project to another?"[2]

Unfortunately, as he acknowledged in the conclusion of his *Diary,* written six months after leaving

Henri Nouwen at the Trappist Abbey of the Genesee

Genesee, it had been an illusion to think that he would emerge from this experience "a different person, more integrated, more spiritual, more virtuous, more compassionate, more gentle, and more joyful."[3]

He traveled to the missions in Latin America, an experience he described in *Gracias!*—another volume of diaries—and even contemplated becoming an affiliate of the Maryknoll Fathers and Brothers. (Recently, I gave a retreat at Maryknoll where the former superior general of that time described how Henri had sought his advice about this plan. He said he had advised Henri that it wasn't the right path for him, and he had always wondered whether that was the correct advice. "Father," I assured him, "that was 100 percent the correct advice!")

Eventually Henri ended up at Harvard Divinity School. This move followed a big celebration at Genesee to celebrate his jubilee as a priest. I was among the many friends he invited. He described his thinking that Genesee would be his base of operations, and he publicly thanked the abbot for providing him, at last, with a true home. The next week Henri called me to say that he was thinking of coming to Harvard. "But I thought that Genesee was going to be your home," I said. "Well," he responded, "the abbot thinks that maybe that is not such a good idea."

So he came to Harvard, where he quickly felt out of place. His lectures attracted enormous crowds, but this celebrity only underlined his abiding sense of loneliness and isolation. Later he wrote with feeling about the temptations that Christ suffered in the desert: to be "relevant, powerful, and spectacular."[4] Behind all this restlessness was an underlying effort to hear God's voice, to find his true home, and to know where he truly belonged.

At this point there came a great turning point in his life. Over the years Nouwen had visited a number of L'Arche communities in France and Canada. In this network of communities, founded by Jean Vanier, mentally disabled adults live together with able helpers. At a time when Henri was feeling himself at a dead-end at Harvard, Jean Vanier invited him to spend a year living at the L'Arche community in France. Perhaps what sealed the deal was Vanier's words: "Maybe we can offer you a home here."

"That, more than anything else," Henri wrote, "was what my heart desired..."[5]

In *The Road to Daybreak,* his journal of that year abroad, Henri wrote movingly of his efforts to adjust

Henri Nouwen with Jean Vanier

to his new home. He begins his diary on a hopeful note: "This is the first day of my new life!" And indeed it was a year of tremendous growth—though marked, as he made it clear, by the same old struggles with rejection, extreme sensitivity, and a propensity to fill every moment with projects and busy-ness. A priest to whom he confided his sense of restlessness told him the obvious: "The issue is not where you are, but how you live wherever you are."[6] That had not changed by the end of his time in France. "I am still the restless, nervous, intense, distracted, and impulse-driven person I was when I set out on this spiritual journey."[7] He still had a long way to go.

In 1986, during his year abroad, he received a formal invitation from Daybreak, the L'Arche community in Toronto, to become their pastor. It was the first time in his life he had received such a formal call. With trepidation he accepted, and Daybreak became his home for the last ten years of his life.

It was unlike anything he had ever known. Nouwen had written extensively about community, but he had never really known community life. That was to change at Daybreak, but it was a struggle. A man of great intellectual gifts, he was physically clumsy and was challenged by such everyday tasks as parking a car or making a sandwich.

At Daybreak, Henri may have assumed that he would be concerned chiefly with pastoral tasks but, like other members of

L'Arche, he was assigned to care for one of the disabled residents—in fact, one of the most severely disabled adults in the community, a young man named Adam, who could not talk or move by himself. Nouwen spent hours each morning simply bathing, dressing, and feeding Adam. Some of his old admirers wondered whether Henri Nouwen was not wasting his talents in such menial duties. But to his surprise he found this an occasion for deep inner conversion. Adam was not impressed by Nouwen's books or his fame or his genius as a public speaker. But through this mute and helpless man, Nouwen began to know what it meant to be "beloved" of God.

This was not, of course, the end of his struggles. After his first year at Daybreak Nouwen suffered an acute nervous breakdown—the culmination of long suppressed tensions. For months he could barely talk or leave his room. Now he was the helpless one, mutely crying out for some affirmation of his existence. As he later described it, "Everything came crashing down—my self-esteem, my energy to live and work, my sense of being loved, my hope for healing, my trust in God ... everything."[8] It was an experience of total darkness, a "bottomless abyss." During these months of anguish, he often wondered if God was real or just a product of his imagination.

But later he wrote, "I now know that while I felt completely abandoned, God didn't leave me alone." With the support of his friends and intensive counseling he was able to break through and to emerge more whole, more at peace with himself. Above all he emerged with a deeper trust in what he called "the inner voice of love," a voice calling him "beyond the boundaries of my short life, to where Christ is all in all."[9]

I had first met Henri in my early years at the Catholic Worker, and our paths had crossed in curious ways. I had spoken with him about becoming a Catholic, and he encouraged me with books to read, including Romano Guardini's *The Lord*. "There is no point in doing this if it is just a matter of changing from one denomination to another," he said. "It has to be because this is how you are being called to grow closer to Jesus."

Our interactions were not always positive. He was deeply hurt when I ended up rejecting an article I had solicited for *The*

Catholic Worker in 1977, judging it "too abstract." Ten years later, when I told him I had been invited to become editor-in-chief at Orbis Books, he told me that he wasn't sure I possessed the "human gifts" for this kind of work. Nevertheless, it was Henri who helped connect me with the Maryknoll Language School in Bolivia, during a post-graduate fellowship (which ultimately led to my work at Orbis), and on my return from Latin America we overlapped at Harvard Divinity School.

In the years that followed my arrival at Orbis in 1987, Henri and I collaborated on various projects, and our work brought us into contact from time to time. He liked to travel with other Daybreak community members, and I could see how relaxed and comfortable he was in their company. In earlier years our relationship had come under strain—in part because of my resistance to his gaping neediness, his constant desire for affirmation, and his frustration that I was not more available as a friend. But this dynamic had changed. He seemed genuinely content and at peace with himself. And this was reflected in his writing, as well. Now when he wrote about community, or peacemaking, or discipleship, or the poor, there was nothing abstract or impersonal about it; he wrote about what he had seen and known firsthand.

In September 1995 he began another "sabbatical year," this time from his work as chaplain to the Daybreak community. "What will I have learned when I finally reach the other end?"[10] he asked himself, in his deeply revealing journal. In typical Nouwen fashion, it proved to be an extremely busy sabbatical, filled with constant travel, meetings, and intense work. In the summer of 1996 Nouwen was working hard, struggling to complete five books. To many friends he seemed happier and more relaxed than they had ever seen him—talking with great enthusiasm of his coming sixty-fifth birthday and plans for the future. Thus it came as a great shock when he suddenly died of a heart attack on September 21, while passing through Amsterdam on his way to work on a documentary in St. Petersburg.

There were numerous ironies at play in this death, the culmination of a "sabbatical" year. Among these was the fact that a man so much afflicted by a sense of homelessness throughout his life should die in his home country, surrounded in the end by his ninety-year-old father and his siblings. The subject of his planned documentary was his favorite painting: Rembrandt's "Return of the Prodigal Son."

But perhaps the surprise should not have been so great. Nouwen's posthumously published *Sabbatical Journey* contains abundant evidence of the terrible fatigue that was tugging at his sleeve, even as a restless energy pushed him forward with plans and projects and the quest for deeper answers. It is hard to believe he was not headed for some culminating experience—whether breakthrough, or collapse, or both. Before Nouwen had set out, his friend Nathan had actually asked what they should do in case of his death—a strangely prescient question to ask a man who was only sixty-four years old. Henri said that he wanted to assure his friends of his gratitude for the life he had lived. He would repeat those same words to Nathan the night before his death.

In fact, Nouwen's writings from the last years of his life indicate how much he had contemplated and prepared for this particular homecoming. In one journal entry he wrote, "How much longer will I live? . . . Only one thing seems clear to me. Every day should be well lived. What a simple truth! Still, it is worth my attention. Did I offer peace today? Did I bring a smile to someone's face? Did I say words of healing? Did I let go of my anger and resentments? Did I forgive? Did I love? These are the real questions! I must trust that the little bit of love that I sow now will bear many fruits, here in this world and in the life to come."[11]

These were not random thoughts, but the reflections of a man who had devoted unusual attention to the prospect of his own death and had adjusted his entire existential attitude accordingly. The central question was not, "How much time remains?" but rather, "How can we prepare for death so that our dying will be a new way for us to send our spirit and God's spirit to those whom we have loved and who have loved us?"[12]

A particular catalyst for Nouwen's reflections came soon after his move to the Daybreak community when he was nearly killed in a traffic accident. As he walked along a busy highway one wintry day, his mind, as usual, on other things, he was struck by the side-view mirror of a passing van. Although it seemed at first that he had suffered only a few broken ribs, it soon emerged that his internal injuries were life threatening. But during this time, as his life hung in the balance, something else happened.

As he later wrote, "I hesitate to speak simply about Jesus, because of my concern that the Name of Jesus might not evoke the full divine presence that I experienced. It was not a warm light, a rainbow, or an open door that I *saw*, but a human yet divine presence that I *felt*, inviting me to come closer and to let go of all fears."[13] As a result, what was on the one hand a terrifying ordeal was also one of the most comforting events of his life. "Death lost its power," he wrote, "and shrank away in the Life and Love that surrounded me in such an intimate way, as if I were walking through a sea whose waves were rolled away. I was being held safe while moving toward the other shore. All jealousies, resentments, and angers were being gently moved away, and I was being shown that Love and Life are greater, deeper, and stronger than any of the forces I had been worrying about."[14]

Anyone familiar with Nouwen's propensity to worry—which is to say, any reader of his previous books—would comprehend the immensity of this statement. In receiving this "gift of peace" Nouwen felt commissioned to share his new awareness with others. Having touched eternity, he now wondered whether his extra years were not given so that he could "live them from the other side," to look at the world "from God's perspective," and "to help others to do the same without their having to be hit by the mirror of a passing van."[15]

In his earlier books Nouwen had taught that our lives belong not just to us but also to others. Now he perceived that this insight applies to our deaths as well. If we die with guilt, shame, anger, or bitterness, all of that becomes part of our legacy to the world, binding and burdening the lives of our family and friends.

It is possible, on the other hand, to regard our dying as a gift—an opportunity to pass along to others our own sense of peace in God.

In many talks on this theme, Nouwen drew on an image taken from his lifelong fascination with the circus. In his later years Nouwen had developed a particular friendship with the Flying Rodleighs, a troupe of trapeze artists whom he had first encountered in a circus in Holland. For a time he even joined them on the road, filling notebooks with his detailed jottings on every aspect of their craft. He entertained the notion of writing a book about the Flying Rodleighs, believing that in their artistry he might find a new vocabulary for the spiritual life.

He had been particularly fascinated by a remark from one of the flyers—the seeming stars of the trapeze act—who told him that, in fact, "the flyer does nothing and the catcher does everything." As the flyer explained, "When I fly to [the catcher] I have simply to stretch out my arms and hands and wait for him to catch me and pull me safely over the apron behind the catch bar... A flyer must fly, and a catcher must catch, and the flyer must trust, with outstretched arms, that his catcher will be there for him."[16]

In this circus wisdom Nouwen found a message of great power and consolation. So often we measure our identity and success by how well we remain in control. But in the end the final meaning of our lives may be determined by our capacity to trust, to let go, to place ourselves in the hands of Another. In this light, he recalled the words of Jesus on the Cross: *Father, into your hands I commend my spirit.* "Dying," he reflected, "is trusting in the catcher."[17]

IN THE LAST MONTHS OF HIS LIFE, Nouwen was shaken by a particular death in the Daybreak community. It was Adam, the severely handicapped young man whom he had cared for during the first year after his arrival at Daybreak; Adam, who had helped him learn, so late in his own life, what it means to be "beloved of God." Finally, after a lifetime of illness and disability, Adam had succumbed to his ailments at the age of thirty-four. For the L'Arche community—which regards its handicapped members as its "core"—Adam's death was a devastating loss. Nouwen rushed back to Toronto from his sabbatical to share the grieving of Adam's family and friends.

Compared to, say, Henri Nouwen, Adam had accomplished nothing, not even the routine tasks that most people take for granted. He could not speak, or dress himself, or brush his own teeth. In the eyes of the world the question would not have been why such a man should die but why God had in the first place permitted him to live. And yet Nouwen saw in Adam's life and death a personal reenactment of the gospel story. As he wrote,

> Adam was—very simply, quietly, and unquietly—there! He was a person who, by his very life, announced the marvelous mystery of our God: I am precious, beloved, whole, and born of God. Adam bore silent witness to this mystery, which has nothing to do with whether or not he could speak, walk, or express himself...It has to do with his being. He was and is a beloved child of God. It is the same news that Jesus came to announce...Life is a gift. Each one of us is unique, known by name, and loved by the One who fashioned us.[18]

Jesus too had accomplished relatively little during his short public life. He too had died as a "failure" in the world's eyes.

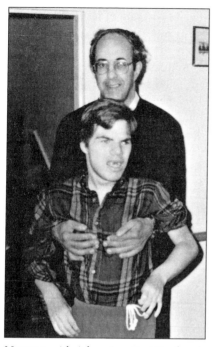

Nouwen with Adam Arnett at Daybreak

"Still," Nouwen wrote, "both Jesus and Adam are God's beloved sons —Jesus by nature, Adam by 'adoption'—and they lived their sonship among us as the only thing that they had to offer. That was their assigned mission. That is also my mission and yours. Believing it and living from it is true sanctity."[19]

Henri was working on a book for me about the Apostles' Creed. He was finding the project more complicated than he had expected. ("I just thought the Apostle's Creed was written by the apostles.") Thus, I was not terribly surprised when he said he wanted to change direction. But I was puzzled by his new plan. "Now hear me out," he said. "It will still be a book about the Creed, but it will be about Adam." Summoning whatever "human gifts" I had acquired over the years, I tried to sound encouraging, though I had no idea what he was talking about. Only as the early drafts began to arrive did I begin to comprehend.

He had chosen to tell the story of Adam according to the narrative pattern of the gospel, describing Adam's "hidden life," his "desert experience" in institutionalization before beginning his public ministry in the L'Arche community, his final passion and death. It might have seemed peculiar to talk about the public mission of a severely disabled man who could not perform the basic tasks of caring for himself. And yet Henri perceived that Adam, like Jesus, had a purpose in life. As was said of Jesus, "'Everyone who touched him was healed.' Each of us who touched Adam has been made whole somewhere."[20]

In the eyes of the world, Adam's life was meaningless—he was a poor, handicapped man, who suffered terrible ill health, was always dependent on others, never able to express his needs or desires, never able to live independently, confined to a small world of dedicated caregivers and family. And yet, in the eyes of faith, as Henri came to see, it was a life of infinite depth and meaning. It was Jesus' story that gave him the eyes to see and the ears to hear the story of Adam's life and death. And it was Adam's story, in turn, that gave Henri the eyes and ears to understand Jesus' story in a new way.

Adam: God's Beloved would be Henri's last book and, as it turned out, I would be his last editor. And this book—as was the case with all of Nouwen's best writing—was also about himself. He seemed to sense in the passing of this young man that he himself was being called to prepare for his own flight into the waiting arms of the Catcher. It was as if, he wrote, Adam was saying, "Don't be afraid, Henri. Let my death help you to befriend yours. When you are no longer afraid of your own death, then you can live fully, freely, and joyfully."[21]

It was a voice he had heard before. In a book that was published shortly after his death he had written, "Many friends and family members have died during the past eight years and my own death is not so far away. But I have heard the inner voice of love, deeper and stronger than ever. I want to keep trusting in that voice, and be led by it beyond the boundaries of my short life, to where Christ is all in all."[22]

LIKE EVERYONE ELSE, I was stunned to receive the news of Henri's death. Just a few weeks before he had come for dinner at my home to drop off the manuscript for *Adam*. I had been so moved by the occasion that I prepared a plaque with the cover of one of his books and sent it to him with a letter thanking him for his years of friendship.

Everything afterward was a blur. His family held a funeral Mass for him in Holland, and then, graciously, arranged for his body to be sent for burial among the Daybreak community in Toronto. I flew up for the day and saw him there for the last time in his open casket—a plain pine box, decorated colorfully by the L'Arche residents. His large hands were at rest—no longer fidgeting.

I was numb, unable to express any thoughts or feelings. But when I returned to work the next day there was an envelope waiting for me in the morning mail, addressed in Henri's unmistakable hand. It was a letter he had written ten days before his death: "Boy oh boy!" he said. "That is quite a plaque! I wonder if there is a humble enough place to hang it without announcing myself too much." He acknowledged his own gratefulness for our friendship and closed with the words, "I look forward to working with you in the years ahead."

It was the first sign that my relationship with Henri was not over. In concluding his book about Adam, Henri had written:

> Is this when his resurrection began, in the midst of my grief? That is what happened to the mourning Mary of Magdala when she heard a familiar voice calling her by her name. That is what happened for the downcast disciples on the road to Emmaus when a stranger talked to them and their hearts burned within them . . . Mourning turns to dancing, grief turns to joy, despair turns to hope, and fear turns to love. Then hesitantly someone is saying, "He is risen, he is risen indeed."[23]

It would be nice to suppose that by the end of his life, Henri had resolved all the complexities of his personality. As his *Sabbatical Journey* makes clear, that was not really the case. "I sometimes wonder how I am going to survive emotionally," he wrote. He acknowledged his inner wound—his "immense need for affection, and this immense fear of rejection." Probably, he recognized, this wound would never go away. It was there to stay. But he had come to a deep insight—that perhaps this wound was "a gateway to my salvation, a door to glory, and a passage to freedom. I am aware that this wound of mine is a gift in disguise. These many short but intense experiences of abandonment lead me to the place where I'm learning to let go of fear and surrender my spirit into the hands of One whose acceptance has no limits."[24]

From Adam he had learned what it means to be beloved of God—which has nothing to do with our talents or special gifts. Jesus had not chosen his disciples because of their exceptional genius or their human gifts. He simply said, "Come follow me." To his disciple Peter he had said: "When you were young you girded yourself and walked where you would; but when you are old, you will stretch out your hands, and another will gird you and lead you where you would not go." Ultimately, trusting the Catcher, Henri had learned to stretch out his hands and let God carry him to the home he had never known in this body.

Henri Nouwen is not the kind of person who is likely to become a candidate for canonization. Yet, for all the broken pieces of his own complex humanity, his life tells a story marked by grace, conversion, and steady growth in the spiritual life. If his work continues, decades after his death, to attract a growing audience, it is not because readers wish to imitate his example or follow his way, but because he helps them to see their own lives in relation to the story of Jesus, as another gospel in the making.

In the end, he did not return from his final journey. But I think that, in his struggle to remain faithful and to trust in God's loving providence, he is the type of restless seeker who opens a path to holiness for all those who struggle amidst life's doubts, unresolved questions, and uncertainties.

6

FLANNERY O'CONNOR
A Companion on the Way

Flannery O'Connor

THERE WON'T BE ANY BIOGRA-
PHIES OF ME," Flannery O'Connor predicted, "for only one
reason, lives spent between the
house and the chicken yard do
not make for exciting copy."[1]
Indeed, her life was lacking in
outward drama—most of it
spent on her mother's dairy
farm in Milledgeville, Georgia,
where she wrote two hours a
day and otherwise cared for her
menagerie of ducks, swans, and
peafowl. Before her death in
1964 she left a relatively small body of work: two short novels
and two collections of short stories. Just that work has been
enough to assure her reputation as one of the greatest American
writers of the twentieth century.

And yet Flannery O'Connor, a devout Catholic, lived in the
confidence that the meaning of our lives cannot ultimately be

From a talk originally delivered as part of the 2004–2005 Series on
Catholic Imagination in Literature at Villanova University. It was pub-
lished as "Flannery O'Connor: Spiritual Master" in *American Catholic
Studies* 116, no. 1 (2005).

measured by outward drama or accomplishments. We were created for a purpose: as the old catechism put it, to "love, honor and serve God in this life so as to be happy with him forever in the next." According to this view, we are pilgrims in this world. And whether our lives are long or short, the meaning is to be found in how faithfully we travel toward our true end.

In that light, Flannery O'Connor has come to function for many people not simply as a great writer of fiction but as a spiritual guide who accompanies and guides us on our own journey; a true spiritual master who invites us to live, as she did, in a world illuminated by the great mysteries of faith.

Doubtless this would come as a surprise to O'Connor herself. She did not set herself up as any kind of example. As she wrote to one correspondent, "I am not a mystic and I do not lead a holy life. Not that I can claim any interesting or pleasurable sins...but I know all about the garden variety, pride, gluttony, envy, and sloth, and what is more to the point my virtues are as timid as my vices."[2]

Her virtues were in fact considerable. But she didn't write to propagate a particular "message," Catholic or otherwise. In fact, to many readers her Catholicism remained a well-kept secret. In contrast to many other Catholic novelists—whether J. F. Powers, Graham Greene, or Mary Gordon—the Catholic world did not supply the setting or "décor" for her stories. Her subjects were more often backwoods fundamentalists, or the "good country people" she encountered among her Georgia neighbors. It was not the settings of her stories but her overall point of view that defined her as a Catholic artist.

Simply, Flannery O'Connor saw the world in light of the great doctrines of her faith: the Fall, the Incarnation, Redemption. That was the world she depicted in her fiction. But as her posthumously published letters make clear, that was also the world she inhabited. In the way she wrote as well as the way she lived she made it possible for many others to experience life from the standpoint of what she called the central Christian mystery: "that it has, for all its horrors, been found worth dying for."[3]

I FIRST ENCOUNTERED O'CONNOR not through her fiction, but through her letters, *The Habit of Being,* a volume edited by her friend Sally Fitzgerald and published in 1979. Her letters bear all the same qualities that *Time* magazine once identified in her first novel: "a brutal irony, a slam-bang humor, and a style of writing as balefully direct as a death sentence." But they display other qualities as well: courage, integrity, hope, an ability to make the life of faith seem not only reasonable and attractive but ultimately necessary.

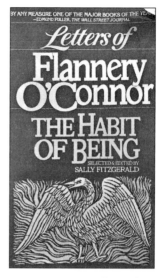

This is what made the greatest impression on me when I first encountered her work many years ago: that for O'Connor, Catholicism was not a matter of believing certain things or even doing certain things but of seeing the world in a certain way. As she said of her work as a writer, "What we roughly call the Catholic novel is not necessarily about a Christianized or Catholicized world, but simply that it is one in which the truth as Christians know it has been used as light to see the world by."[4]

She eschewed most labels—even that of "Catholic novelist." But she did call herself a "Christian Realist."[5] This reflected her conviction, as a Christian, that she lived in the presence of certain theological truths. These were not simply matters of subjective belief; they were part of the nature of Reality, as solid as the laws of physics. And this was so regardless of whether anyone else noticed or shared her beliefs. As she said, "The truth does not change according to our ability to stomach it emotionally"—or, as she might have added, to understand it rationally.[6]

She was quite aware of the fact that most people in the modern age—at least, most of the people who read her stories—did not share her beliefs. Her audience, as she wrote, was made up of "the kind of people who think God is dead."[7] This tension posed a particular challenge to her vocation as a writer. How to convey the reality of such principles as sin and grace to an audience inclined to regard these words as "twin idiocies"? In one of her letters she posed this challenge simply: for the Christian writer "the ultimate reality is the Incarnation, the present reality is the Incarnation, and nobody believes in the Incarnation."[8]

To get this vision across to a "hostile audience" she often resorted to violent literary means—shock, distortion, exaggeration: "to the hard of hearing you shout, and for the almost-blind you draw large and startling figures."[9]

In one of her letters, O'Connor wrote,

> I don't think you should write something as long as a novel around anything that is not of the gravest concern to you and everybody else, and for me this is always the conflict between an attraction for the Holy and the disbelief in it that we breathe in with the air of our times. It's hard to believe always but more so in the world we live in now. There are some of us who have to pay for our faith every step of the way and who have to work out dramatically what it would be like without it and if being without it would be ultimately possible or not.[10]

That is a pretty good description of the concerns treated in her first novel, *Wise Blood*, which she wrote when she was in her early twenties.

Like many of her later stories, *Wise Blood* is inhabited by a cast of bizarre characters, including a guitar-strumming snake-oil salesman; a phony prophet who has pretended to blind himself; and the central character, Hazel Motes, whom O'Connor called a "Christian *malgre lui*" (despite himself), a kind of Jonah figure, who goes to extreme lengths to avoid his destiny as one of God's prophets. It is a comic novel, which in O'Connor's view meant serious business—"for all comic novels that are any good must be about matters of life and death."[11]

The existence of an objective order of sin and grace, disguised under the cloak of mystery, is the underlying assumption of her novel. Early in *Wise Blood* O'Connor, with shades of Dante, describes a night sky "underpinned with long silver streaks that looked like scaffolding and depth on depth behind it were thousands of stars that all seemed to be moving very slowly as if they were about some vast construction work that involved the whole order of the universe and would take all time to complete." The problem is, "no one was paying attention to the sky."[12]

There is O'Connor's Christian Realism: the apprehension that the universe is part of a vast construction project that takes all time to complete—regardless of whether anyone is paying any attention—and that the meaning of our own small but unique lives is to find our place in that cosmic drama.

In the case of Hazel (or Haze) Motes, it is matter of claiming his destiny to be a prophet of Jesus. At the beginning of the novel he has determined to run as far from this fate as possible. The image of Jesus instilled in him by his grandfather is menacing: a "wild ragged figure motioning him to turn around and come off into the dark where he was not sure of his footing, where he might be walking on the water and not know it and then suddenly know it and drown."[13] To escape from that image he denies not only the reality of Christ but the set of assumptions and consequences that surround such belief: sin, mystery, the need for redemption—the existence of an objective, moral universe and the personal responsibility that that implies.

What sets Haze apart from everyone around him—and what saves him in the long run—is his sense of ultimate urgency. Whether Jesus exists or doesn't is a question of unique importance. Either way one must accept all the implications down to the letter. If Christ does not exist, life is essentially meaningless and one must create one's own rules. If Christ does not exist, then sin does not exist, there being no one to sin against. In that case all that matters "is that Jesus is a liar."[14]

In other words, Haze doesn't just blend in with the crowd of happy agnostics. He becomes an anti-preacher, the soap-box evangelist of his own religion, which he calls "The Church without Christ": that is, the "church where the blind don't see and the lame don't walk and what's dead stays that way."[15]

Not only by his "preaching" but by his bold sinning Haze does everything he can to defy God. Ultimately, however, he finds it impossible to sustain this nihilism. In spite of himself he finds it impossible to deny his sense of personal responsibility. There is indeed an objective moral universe, whether he wants to believe it or not. If that is so, then Jesus is real. And if that is so, then he is nothing but a sinner. Fanatic that he is, he carries out his own judgment and blinds himself.

Summarized in such a manner, this book certainly does not sound hopeful. But Hazel's mission and his journey do not end with this self-inflicted violence. His journey continues, with intimations of a much more merciful and loving God than he could have previously imagined.

At this point, however, we move outside of Hazel's mind and see the action entirely through the viewpoint of Mrs. Flood, the perplexed and suspicious landlady who cares for him. Through her eyes, trained skeptically on the man who is now blind, Hazel, we begin to perceive that there is a different dimension to life, an order of Reality that is deeper and wider than the world she has been living in.

> To her the blind man had the look of seeing something. His face had a peculiar pushing look, as if it were going forward after something it could just distinguish in the distance...she didn't get rid of the feeling that she was being cheated. Why had he destroyed his eyes and saved himself unless he had some plan, unless he saw something that he couldn't get without being blind to everything else?
>
> He might as well be one of them monks, she thought, he might as well be in a monkery. She didn't understand it. She didn't like the thought that something

was being put over her head. She liked the clear light of day. She liked to see things.[16]

When Mrs. Flood tries to picture what it must be like inside the blind man's head,

> she imagined it was like you were walking in a tunnel and all you could see was a pin point of light. She had to imagine the pin point of light; she couldn't think of it at all without that. She saw it as some kind of a star, like the star on Christmas cards. She saw him going backwards to Bethlehem and she had to laugh...[17]

This theme of sight-in-blindness continues to the very end of the novel as Hazel Motes lies dying.

> The outline of a skull was plain under his skin and the deep burned eye sockets seemed to lead into a dark tunnel where he had disappeared. She leaned closer and closer to his face, looking deep into them, trying to see how she had been cheated or what had cheated her, but she couldn't see anything. She shut her eyes and saw the pin point of light but so far away that she could not hold it steady in her mind. She felt as if she were blocked at the entrance of something. She sat staring with her eyes shut, into his eyes, and felt as if she had finally got to the beginning of something she couldn't begin, and she saw him moving farther and farther away, farther and farther into the darkness until he was the pin point of light.[18]

In other words, by the end of the novel Hazel has assumed his place as one small star in that great construction project in the heavens. And at least one person has finally taken notice.

SOON AFTER FINISHING THIS NOVEL O'Connor's life was drastically affected by the discovery that she suffered from lupus, the same disease that had killed her father. Her illness imposed severe limitations on her ability to work, ultimately forcing her to walk on crutches and hastening her death at the age of thirty-nine.

She accepted her condition with grace, even coming to see her outward constraints as contributing to her vocation as an artist: "I have enough energy to write with," she said, "and as that is all I have any business doing anyhow, I can with one eye squinted take it all as a blessing. What you have to measure out, you come to observe closer, or so I tell myself."[19] From the great Jesuit scientist and mystic, Pierre Teilhard de Chardin, she borrowed the phrase "passive diminishment."[20] This referred to the fact that our spiritual character is formed as much by what we endure and what is taken from us as it is by our achievements and our conscious choices. This was the same drama depicted in the life of so many of her fictional characters as they are stripped of their sins and even their evident "virtues" in order to receive a deeper truth.

Overall, O'Connor understood that her particular vocation as an artist was subsumed in the larger vocation shared by every Christian: "to prepare his death in Christ."[21] In this journey toward what she called her "true country" she was assisted by scripture, the sacraments, and the convictions of her faith, as well as the support and prayers of her friends.

Here, again, her letters reveal just how much her personal circumstances, her sharp intelligence, and her deeply held faith combined to forge a prophetic vision of extraordinary depth. And here I have to speak about my own discovery of O'Connor's work and the part she played in my own journey.

When, during my break from college at the age of nineteen, I made my way to the Catholic Worker in New York City, I was not motivated by explicitly religious concerns. I was basically attracted to the Catholic Worker because of its nonviolent activism—especially the pictures of Dorothy Day getting arrested with the farmworkers or protesting civil defense drills in the 1950s.

I knew that Day's life was rooted in prayer, in daily Mass, in saying the rosary, and in her devotion to the saints. But all this meant nothing to me. In the light of that, it was surprising that after a few months Dorothy asked me to become the managing editor of the Catholic Worker paper, a job I performed for two years. Some may find it notable that I took on this job without being a Catholic, though at the time it didn't seem like a big deal.

I had come to feel at home in the religious language of the Catholic Worker, without feeling any particular need to relate to a wider church. The Catholic Worker was my church, as far as I was concerned. Here was the true church—living with the poor, marching on picket lines, going to jail.

This was of course very far from Dorothy's understanding—and a sign of how little I really understood her. But at a certain point it all caught up with me. I couldn't sustain this life on the strength of my own virtue or good intentions. It all came crashing down and I felt desperately that I couldn't continue.

I took a job that was in many ways providential: working the night shift as an orderly in a home for terminal cancer patients. St. Rose's home was run by an order of Dominican nuns founded by the daughter of Nathaniel Hawthorne. It was a different kind of Catholic environment, very traditional by Catholic Worker standards—or any standards, for that matter. The nuns wore white habits; statues of St. Joseph and St. Therese adorned the hallways. Every morning the nuns began their day with the Eucharist, which was broadcast throughout the wards.

And here I was, all alone each night from 1:00 to 8:00 AM on the men's floor, walking the darkened corridors, emptying catheter bags or changing diapers on incontinent patients; talking to men if they woke up and wanted company; sitting beside them as they died; and then washing their bodies and carting them to the morgue.

I had a lot of time to myself. In fact, this whole nocturnal routine tended to put me on a different schedule from the rest of the world. It was a kind of retreat. I found myself reading spiritual classics, like the *Confessions* of St. Augustine, and Pascal's *Pensées*, along with novels by writers like Georges Bernanos, François Mauriac, and Graham Greene. And I found myself comforted by the world they described.

And then one day I read a review of a new collection of letters by Flannery O'Connor: *The Habit of Being*. I bought a copy of the book and read it from cover to cover. Then I started over again. Then I read through all her stories and novels. Then I read all the books that she mentioned in her letters. At first it was no more than a pin-point of light, but the more I read the more I found things coming into a new focus.

In a review of *The Habit of Being* that I wrote for *Sojourners* magazine I noted that "Flannery O'Connor was one of those who could not be a Christian without being first of all a Roman Catholic." And as I wrote those words I realized that the same was true for me. What was it in reading O'Connor that brought me to this conviction in a way that years at the Catholic Worker had not?

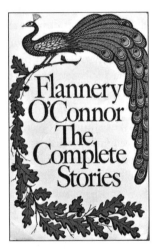

Of course, there probably could not be a setting more conducive to the study of Flannery O'Connor than this: surrounded by men in various stages of dying. So many of O'Connor's stories have to do with moments of epiphany or revelation that break into the settled everyday existence of people who are oblivious to their own sinfulness and their need for conversion. Sometimes it comes about through violence. In her story, "A Good Man is Hard to Find," a silly old grandmother comes to her moment of truth just before she is shot by an escaped criminal known as The Misfit. The Misfit says, "She would have been a good woman if she had only had someone to shoot her every day of her life."[22]

Of course O'Connor herself lived close to the reminder of death. But by a further coincidence she had a special connection with the very order of nuns who ran the hospice I was working in: the Hawthorne Dominicans. (Several of the older nuns I worked with remembered meeting her.) At the urging of this community, which operated one of their homes for terminal cancer patients in Atlanta, she had written the introduction to a biography of a little girl named Mary Ann, who had died of cancer at the age of twelve after spending most of her short life among the nuns.[23]

O'Connor used the life and death of this little girl to reflect on the meaning of human life as a preparation for our final end. The meaning of a life is not measured in what we do or achieve but in the quality of our hearts or souls—the way we use our lives, whether long or short, to advance our progress toward our true end.

In our culture we put so much emphasis on youthfulness and longevity and so little on discovering the real purpose or destination of life. Death is so often a sad topic that we try to hide away or avoid. Doctors struggle valiantly to keep people alive as long as possible and often feel defeated when their efforts fail. It is as if death is some kind of unfortunate accident, rather than a reality that is sewn into the basic fabric of our existence.

For O'Connor and for many other Christian saints, the basic question is not why we die, but why we live. What is the purpose of this life that ends inevitably in death? Of course, the Christian answer is that death is not the end, and this makes a great deal of difference. I could see this in the nuns at St. Rose's Home and in so many of the patients.

I was surrounded by an atmosphere of death—the stench of cancer and incontinence... But I was also surrounded by a different atmosphere—of faith, love, grace, a sense that it was a privilege and an honor to be able to accompany people in this ultimate and most meaningful passage of life. The presence of death only underscored the preciousness of life. And so, often, upon staggering into the sunshine after another night on the ward, I found myself feeling not just exhausted but also exhilarated.

Flannery O'Connor died at the age of thirty-nine. But she was alive in the fullest sense of the word, so acute was her understanding of the meaning and purpose of life in its wholeness and holiness.

This was part of what I perceived in O'Connor. But there was more.

I had always thought of Catholicism as a matter of believing certain things: the fact that Jesus is God, for instance; or, through my work at the Catholic Worker, that it is a matter of doing certain things, a certain morality.

It was from Flannery O'Connor that I first comprehended that faith is a matter of seeing the world in a different way and endeavoring to live in the light of that vision. This was a revelation. What would it mean to live as if the doctrines of faith were true? How would we see the world differently? This certainly provided the moral framework in O'Connor's fiction, and I could see that it also provided the spiritual framework in which she lived: "I feel that if I were not a Catholic, I would have no reason to write, no reason to see, no reason ever to feel horrified or even to enjoy anything."[24]

And finally, from O'Connor I received a larger view of what it means to belong to the church—a spiritual communion of saints and sinners that is both Mother and Teacher and, at the same time, in some mystical sense, the Body of Christ. O'Connor's letters are marked throughout by a deep love for the church that was able to accommodate a clear-eyed apprehension of its sins and failures. This tension is well reflected in her statement, "I think that the Church is the only thing that is going to make the terrible world we are coming to endurable; the only thing that makes the Church endurable is that it is somehow the body of Christ and that on this we are fed."[25]

In her correspondence O'Connor often assumes the role of besieged Defender of the Faith. Both as a Catholic in the heart of the Protestant South and as a believer in dialogue with the culture of skepticism, O'Connor felt the constant challenge, as St. Paul would put it, to "account for the faith and hope within her." Certainly this forced her to sharpen and clarify her thinking. As much as any Hyde Park evangelist, she was skilled in addressing questions about the Incarnation, the Eucharist, the difference between the Virgin Birth and the Immaculate Conception, papal infallibility, and the usual catalog of Catholic sins (the Inquisition, the condemnation of Galileo, the vulgarity of the Catholic press, etc.). At the same time, her letters reflect the efforts of a thinking

Catholic to bring her faith into dialogue with the burning questions of the day—"to feel the contemporary situation at the ultimate level."[26]

At the time of her death in 1964, the Second Vatican Council
(1962–1965) was still in progress in Rome. Evidently its impact
had not yet penetrated as far as Milledgeville, Georgia. Her letters
contain surprisingly few references to this monumental event in
the life of the church, and little sense of how soon many of the
comfortable certainties of American Catholic culture would be
swept away.

One can assume she would have welcomed the pastoral spirit
Pope John bequeathed to the church. As one critic has put it, she
was "a one-woman *aggiornamento*."[27] Her favorite writers were
figures like Romano Guardini, Pierre Teilhard de Chardin, and
other counterparts from an earlier era—Baron von Hügel, and
Cardinal Newman—who had struggled to enlarge the space for
a certain intellectual freedom in the church. At the same time she
was critical of a type of liberalizing pressure to make Catholicism
more acceptable to the rational mind. That way, she believed, lay
the "vaporization" of religion. When the church was stripped of
its mystery, she feared, it was liable to become just another "Elks
Club."[28]

Among her constant themes—the most perplexing to her liberal friends—was the importance of dogma. Rather than limiting
freedom of belief, she regarded dogma as an essential safeguard
of mystery. It preserved the sense of something "larger than
human understanding." This was a tremendous boon to the
writer, who was not forced to "invent" her own reality. But it
also had wider implications: "Those who have no absolute values
cannot let the relative remain merely relative; they are always
raising it to the level of the absolute."[29]

Reading Flannery O'Connor was really an intense course in
the heart and spirit of Catholicism. The outcome of this course
came on Holy Thursday in 1980 when I was received into the
Catholic Church.

That was not the end of my journey. Nor was it the end of my
debt to Flannery O'Connor. Among other things she led me to

Sally Fitzgerald, her friend and the editor of *The Habit of Being*, to whom I addressed a shy fan letter, thus eliciting this reply:

> I was overjoyed to hear that you had been received into the Church. I remember always the distinction that Flannery made: "One doesn't *join* the Catholic Church; one becomes a Catholic."[30] It is a long process, I have found, as a convert myself. I am still trying to get there, and getting even to this point has been in every way worth it. So, I wish you a happy beginning and (or to) an even happier end. It must please Flannery enormously to know that her letters could serve as a kind of catalyst to your realization of the *reality* at the core of Catholicism. I feel very lucky to have had a part in getting them to you, and to everyone else who has recognized their meaning.

This was the beginning of a long and valued friendship that lasted until Sally's death from cancer many years later. I had asked her to edit an anthology of Flannery O'Connor's writings for a series I was launching on "Modern Spiritual Masters"—a task she accepted. When illness made it impossible for her to undertake this project, I offered to edit the book myself. I sent the manuscript to her, hoping she might still find it possible to write an introduction. That manuscript was by her bedside, two days later, when she died. The experience of working on the project offered an opportunity to look back over my own journey and the thread leading back to the young man, myself, who first responded to these writings.

In many ways my perspective on Catholicism had changed. I found it hard to identify with O'Connor's pre-Vatican II triumphalism. Her condescending attitude toward Protestants, her deference to religious authority, her tendency to identify Catholicism as the Truth with a capital T—much of this seemed a relic of a bygone era.

But other things came through even more clearly for me. For instance, the tenderness and compassion with which she addressed a college student who was struggling with his faith:

I think that this experience you are having of losing your faith, or as you think, of having lost it, is an experience that in the long-run belongs to faith; or at least it can belong to faith if faith is still valuable to you…

I don't know how the kind of faith required of a Christian living in the 20th century can be at all if it is not grounded on this experience that you are having right now of unbelief. This may be the case always and not just in the 20th century. Peter said, "Lord I believe. Help my unbelief." It is the most natural and most human and most agonizing prayer in the gospels, and I think it is the foundation prayer of faith…

Even in the life of a Christian, faith rises and falls like the tides of an invisible sea. It's there, even when he can't see it or feel it, if he wants it be there. You realize, I think that it is more valuable, more mysterious, altogether more immense than anything you can learn or decide upon in college. Learn what you can, but cultivate Christian skepticism. It will keep you free—not free to do anything you please, but free to be formed by something larger than your own intellect or the intellects of those around you.[31]

Or the courage and grace with which she contended with her own infirmities: "I have never been anywhere but sick. In a sense sickness is a place, more instructive than a long trip to Europe, and it's always a place where there's no company, where nobody can follow. Sickness before death is a very appropriate thing and I think those who don't have it miss one of God's mercies."[32]

Though I have traveled a long way in my own journey of faith, I continue to hold on to Flannery O'Connor, and to so many other spiritual guides whom I met through her, as true companions on my way. At the time of my first encounter with O'Connor I resonated with her description of conversion as "a kind of blasting annihilating light, a light that will last a lifetime."[33] But as I have grown older I recognize also what she meant when she called it an evolving process—a matter of "continually turning toward God and away from your own egocentricity."[34]

Like many other Christians, O'Connor held an understanding of the human condition as a kind of pilgrimage. This offered some explanation for the dilemma of our lives—our frequent feelings of alienation and estrangement. But it also offered the promise that our life has a meaning and a goal, a hope that if we travel by faith we will find the way to our true country.

My experience has been that we benefit from companions and guides on that journey. Flannery O'Connor has served that role for me. But in the desire for such companionship she was no different.

O'Connor clipped out a prayer to St. Raphael that she found printed in the *Catholic Worker*. She told one of her correspondents that she uttered this prayer every day of her life. St. Raphael, the archangel, leads us to the people we are supposed to meet.

> *O Raphael, lead us toward those we are waiting for, those who are waiting for us: Raphael, Angel of happy meeting, lead us by the hand toward those we are looking for. May all our movements be guided by your Light and transfigured by your joy.*
>
> *Angel, guide of Tobias, lay the request we now address to you at the feet of Him on whose unveiled Face you are privileged to gaze. Lonely and tired, crushed by the separations and sorrows of life, we feel the need of calling you and of pleading for the protection of your wings, so that we may not be as strangers in the province of joy, all ignorant of the concerns of our country. Remember the weak, you who are strong, you whose home lies beyond the region of thunder, in a land that is always peaceful, always serene and bright with the resplendent glory of God.[35]*

7

CHARLES DE FOUCAULD
Little Brother

ON THE EVENING OF DECEMBER 1, 1916, Charles de Foucauld
was roused from his prayers by an urgent knock on the door of
his hermitage in Tamanrasset, a remote outpost in the Saharan
desert of Algeria. Foucauld, the only Catholic priest within many
hundreds of miles, was known as the Marabout, or holy man. It
was a mark of respect on the part of his Tuareg neighbors. Devout Muslims, they respected the Frenchman's piety and good
works, though they were not tempted to share his faith.

Despite the isolation of his hermitage, Brother Charles was
accustomed to receiving visitors at all hours. Part of his mission
as a "little brother of Jesus" was to remain available to the needs
of his neighbors. But lately he had taken unusual precautions.
The reverberations of the Great War in Europe were being felt
even in this isolated corner of the desert. He had been warned
that Tuareg rebels, inspired by a brotherhood of Muslim fanatics,
might be looking for an opportunity to strike a blow against the
French infidels. Thus he had lately fortified his hermitage, and
he did not answer a knock at the door without determining the
identity of his caller.

The desert sand had muffled the sound of camels and the dismounting of the forty armed men who now surrounded his little

---

An earlier version of this essay appeared in *Martyrs: Contemporary
Writers on Modern Lives of Faith*, ed. Susan Bergman (San Francisco:
HarperCollins, 1996; Maryknoll, NY: Orbis Books, 1998) and as the
introduction to *Charles de Foucauld: Selected Writings*, ed. Robert Ellsberg (Maryknoll, NY: Orbis Books, 1999).

fort. The caller identified himself as the mailman. In fact he was a local tribesman, known to Charles, who had accepted a bribe to transact this betrayal. Trustingly, Charles unbolted the door and reached out his hand, only to be roughly seized. The rebels poured in and bound his arms. While some of them subjected him to interrogation, others searched the hermitage for valuables. Charles did not answer their questions, but only seemed to pray silently while a fifteen-year-old boy pressed a rifle against his temple. When twenty minutes had elapsed a noise was heard, the sound of two approaching camels. Charles started to move, whereupon his frightened guard shot the priest through the head.

FOUCAULD'S LONELY DEATH WAS IN CHARACTER with the solitude and obscurity of his life. He had spent years in the desert preparing the way for followers who never arrived, and his efforts had ended this way, with a shot in the dark, a sound quickly absorbed by the cold sand of the surrounding dunes. Compared to the rivers of blood then flowing through Europe, it was a relatively unremarkable event. No one could have anticipated the extent of his later influence, the fact that several congregations would trace their foundation to his inspiration, that indeed Charles de Foucauld would come to be regarded as one of the most significant religious figures of the twentieth century. But in fact the path between his death and his later influence is far less remarkable than the path that led to his final appointment in Tamanrasset.

Viscount Charles-Eugène de Foucauld was born in Strasbourg on September 15, 1858, to a proudly aristocratic family. Throughout his childhood he was regaled with stories of his ancestors' honor and of their history of service to cross and crown. The Foucaulds, he learned, had fought in the Crusades and stood beside Joan of Arc at Orleans, thus earning the family a title and a coat of arms emblazoned with a heroic motto: "Never Retreat." Of the varieties of valor, however, his pious mother paid special tribute to the example of Armand de Foucauld, archbishop of Arles, who had died a martyr during the revolutionary terror of 1792. But Charles's mother was given little time to impart her faith and ideals. She died in childbirth when Charles was six, a loss compounded only six months later by his father's death from tuberculosis.

Charles and his younger sister were entrusted to the care of their maternal grandfather, a retired colonel already in his seventies. The colonel excelled in discipline, and he had great hopes as his grandson matured that the boy would carry on the family tradition. But for Charles such hopes were not sufficient to fill the yawning void he felt within. Lacking any wider purpose or ambition, he turned increasingly to frivolous diversions and the indulgence of his considerable appetite. He had little interest in his studies. Any religious faith he might once have known had been casually discarded along the way. Nevertheless, to oblige his grandfather he agreed to apply to the military academy of Saint-Cyr. With special tutoring he managed just to squeeze through the entrance examinations—allowance being made for his family name. No special connections, however, could help him squeeze his overfed body into a regulation uniform. For this a private tailor had to be commissioned. This was why, in later years—even when he had become a scrawny hermit—he would be affectionately known by his comrades in the elite officer corps as "Piggy."

Charles looked resplendent in his uniform. But the uniform did not make the cadet. His years in the academy were distin-

Lieutenant Charles de Foucauld

guished only by the frequency of his official reprimands. It might be supposed that such a figure would earn the disdain of the more disciplined cadets. In fact he carried off his escapades with such *joie d'esprit* that he seems instead to have endeared himself to his classmates, many of whom would remain his lifelong friends. As one of them later recalled, "If you have not seen Foucauld in his room, clad in his white flannel pajamas buttoned with frogs, sprawled leisurely on his divan or in a commodious armchair, enjoying a tasty snack of *pâté de fois gras*, washing it down with a choice champagne, then you have never seen a man really enjoying himself."

By this time, following his grandfather's death, Charles had come into a considerable fortune—the better to underwrite his epicurean tastes. His room became the site of extravagant entertainments. He was generous in sharing the contents of his wine cellar and the services of his personal barber. But occasionally he went too far. One time he slipped off base in disguise, defying a confinement to quarters, in order to keep a dinner engagement with his mistress, a certain Mimi. When the ruse was discovered and he faced his superiors he explained that he could hardly do otherwise—a commitment to a young woman was a matter of honor. This was not the military definition of honor, but for sheer audacity it apparently won passing marks. He managed to escape with a severe reprimand.

From Saint-Cyr Charles was passed on to cavalry school. There he graduated in 1879, eighty-sixth in a class of eighty-seven. The inspector general described him as "a remarkable person . . . with no thought for anything except entertainment." His first posting was to North Africa, where he quickly got into trouble for sending Mimi on ahead, passing her off as the Viscountess de Foucauld. In light of the ensuing scandal Charles was informed that he must make a choice—either Mimi or the army. Without hesitation he made his choice: he resigned his commission and returned to France and to his scandalized family. They retaliated by putting his finances into the hands of a trustee.

He had scarcely arrived in Paris, however, when he applied to rejoin his old unit. News had reached him that his comrades were about to go into battle against Arab rebels and he could not bear the thought of sitting on the sidelines. And so he bade farewell to Mimi—this time forever—and returned to Algeria.

This was to be the turning point for Foucauld, the moment when a different side of his personality began to emerge. To everyone's surprise, he fought valiantly in battle and demonstrated considerable skill as an officer. The more lasting effect of this experience, however, was a new fascination with the North African desert and its people. After only six months in active service, long enough to rehabilitate his honor, Charles again resigned his commission to pursue an ambitious and dangerous mission. He had decided to undertake a one-man geographical expedition to Morocco, a vast territory as yet unexplored by Western outsiders. Because of the risks facing any lone Christian in this Muslim country, Charles disguised himself as a wandering Jewish rabbi. For eleven months he traveled the country, armed only with a sextant and compass, finally emerging with the material for a book. When it was published in 1885 he was awarded the gold medal of the French Geographical Society.

Back in Paris, Charles's family was delighted by his new demonstration of discipline and purpose. But already his restless heart was stirring in a new direction. The experience of Muslim piety had made a lasting impression on Charles, and he found himself increasingly drawn to the religion of his youth. As he wrote, "My exposure to this faith [Islam] and to the soul living always in God's presence helped me understand that there is something greater and more real than the pleasures of this world."

An irresistible force was drawing him, where he could not say. But over and over, as he restlessly roamed the streets of Paris, he repeated a prayer: "My God, if you exist, make your existence known to me." In the fall of 1886, after having finally overcome his inhibitions, he made his way to the church of St. Augustine, where he sought out Abbé Huvelin, a famous confessor and spiritual director. Finding Huvelin in his confessional, he described his predicament and asked the priest to recommend some Christian reading. Huvelin, with inspired insight into the character of this seeker, told Charles that what he needed was not to be found in books. All that he needed to do was make his confession, receive communion, and he would believe. Charles complied, and at once he felt his life transformed. He left the church of St. Augustine that day determined to give himself entirely to God. As he wrote later, "As soon as I believed there was a God, I understood that I could not do anything other than live for him. My religious vocation dates from the same moment as my faith."

The confessional at the Church of St. Augustine in Paris where Charles de Foucaulds's life was tranformed

The question for Charles now was what form this vocation should take. At the suggestion of Huvelin—into whose hands he had fully entrusted himself—Charles undertook a pilgrimage to the Holy Land. There he spent several months visiting the holy shrines and following the footsteps of Jesus in the actual towns and countryside where he had walked. This experience would ultimately have a decisive impact on his life. But all that was clear at this point was his determination to embrace a life of prayer and poverty. The austere Trappist order seemed to offer the best means of fulfilling this calling. And so Charles renounced his fortune, applied to the Trappists, and eventually settled in a monastery in Syria, the most remote and impoverished community he could find.

Charles dutifully applied himself to the discipline of monastic life. He stuck it out for more than seven years. But it did not satisfy his yearning. For one thing, it fell short of his imagined ideal of poverty. Despite the famous rigors of the Trappist life, Charles found it altogether too comfortable. "We are poor in the eyes of the rich," he wrote, "but not so poor as Our Lord was." When a papal order slightly mitigated the Trappist dietary rules to allow a bit of oil or butter on their vegetables, Charles was indignant: "A little less mortification means so much less offered to the Good Lord; a little more spent on feeding us means so much less to give the poor...Where will it all stop?" When he was once sent on a pastoral errand to the hovel of an Arab Christian who was dying of cholera, Charles was appalled to see the contrast between the dignified simplicity of the monastery and the actual poverty of a common peasant.

At the same time Charles had begun to question whether it was really to any traditional monastic life that he was being called. Increasingly he was haunted by an insight from his sojourn in the Holy Land. What impressed him then was the realization that Jesus, though the Son of God, had lived most of his life as a poor man and a worker. As a carpenter in Nazareth Jesus had, in these lowly circumstances, embodied the gospel message in its entirety before ever announcing it in words. From this insight it occurred to Charles that the "hidden life" of Nazareth, and not the monastery, should be the model for his own spirituality.

It took a while for Charles to obtain a dispensation from the Trappists; he was at this point within months of making his final vows. Huvelin, too, was reluctant to endorse Charles's impetuous plan. But eventually Charles was free to return to the Holy Land, to Nazareth itself, where he found a position as a servant at a convent of Poor Clares. Calling himself simply Brother Charles, he spent three happy years in this occupation, dividing his waking hours between his minimal chores and a far more rigorous schedule of prayer. He exulted in the thought that he was living in the same place where Jesus had spent thirty years of his life and where "I have now the unutterable, the inexpressibly profound happiness of raking manure."

But though Charles aspired to emulate the "hidden life" of Jesus, his evident holiness eventually attracted the attention of the mother superior of the Poor Clares. She convinced Charles that he had a more important mission to perform in the world and urged him to become a priest. Though Charles felt unworthy of ordination, he found himself exhilarated by the dream of founding a community of likeminded brothers. Once again Charles turned to the counsel of Huvelin, who expressed his opinion in blunt terms: "You are not made, not at all made, to lead others." Nevertheless he helped arrange for Charles to return to France to undergo seminary training.

Shortly after his ordination in 1901 Charles returned once more to North Africa. To live out his new mission, he had concluded, it was no longer necessary to reside in the actual town of Nazareth. "Nazareth" might be any place. And so he returned to Algeria, to the oasis of Béni-Abbès on the border of Morocco. His goal was to develop a new model of contemplative religious life, a community of "Little Brothers," who would live among the poor in a spirit of service and solidarity. In the constitutions he devised for his planned order he wrote, "The whole of our existence, the whole of our lives should cry the Gospel from the rooftops...not by our words but by our lives." He was now forty-two, ready at last to begin his true mission.

Béni-Abbès was a predominantly Arab settlement, though also the site of a French garrison. As a French colony, Algeria was administered under military authority. Since it was the policy of the French government to avoid any provocation of the Muslim population, Charles could hardly have established his hermitage without approval from the military authorities. But here, and not for the last time, his old connections proved invaluable. Many of his classmates from the academy had risen to positions of authority in the colonies, and they were only too willing to assist a former comrade—even one whose career had taken such an unlikely turn.

Ostensibly Charles's mission was to divide his time between service to the Arabs and pastoral duties among the garrisoned troops. He was the only priest within 250 miles. Thus, a good deal of his time was spent saying Mass and hearing the soldiers' confessions. But his heart was with the mass of his Arab neighbors to whom Christ was as yet unknown. He dressed like one of them in a coarse white robe, with a leather belt around his waist. His only distinguishing marks were the rosary tucked in his belt and an emblem of his own design—a red heart with a cross—sewn over his breast. His aim was not to convert the Arabs, but rather to offer a Christian presence in their midst.

Ultimately Charles regarded himself as simply the advance agent for a community of Little Brothers. But no followers ever came. There were not many at the time who could even comprehend his novel approach to mission, and fewer still who could endure the extreme, nearly impossible, standards of asceticism

Charles de Foucauld at Béni-Abbès

that Charles embraced. He had traveled far from the days when he had lounged on a sofa, feasting on oysters and pâté. Now he worked hard by day, spent half the night in prayer, slept on the bare ground, and subsisted on a diet of dates and boiled barley. His former abbot, one of those to whom he frequently appealed for helpers, was realistic in observing: "I fear he would drive a disciple mad by excessive mental concentration before killing him by excessive austerities."

After several years in Béni-Abbès Charles began to find the isolated outpost too congested for his taste. In 1905, on the lookout for a more remote setting, he accepted an invitation from Colonel Henri Laperrine, an old classmate and now the commander of the Saharan Oases, to tag along on an expedition to the Saharan interior. Thus Charles discovered the rugged Hoggar region—a barren plateau surrounded by dramatic volcanic mountains, deep in the heart of the desert. Charles was enchanted by the complete isolation of the region and by its mysterious inhabitants, the Tuaregs. They were a semi-nomadic people, famous for their ardor in battle, easily recognized by their peculiar complexion, their skin dyed blue from the color of their distinctive veils. If he were to live in the Hoggar he would be the only priest within sixty days of desert travel. The attraction was irresistible. He decided at once to move his hermitage there to the village of Tamanrasset. Laperrine, for his part, had hoped for such an outcome; it pleased him to imagine that through this priest a bridge might be formed to the remote tribal peoples of the Saharan interior. Who was better equipped for such a mission than Piggy?

His new home, Tamanrasset, was hardly a village at all. Twenty families lived in this settlement, halfway up a mountain at an elevation of 4,600 feet. A small oasis nourished a few tufts of grass and sustained the meager gardens and small herds of goats on which the people subsisted. By day the sun was mercilessly bright, with temperatures reaching 110 degrees. At sunset the mountain tops caught fire in a crimson blaze. By night the temperature could drop 70 degrees, while the sky was illuminated by a sea of stars. With time Charles came to know that sky so well that he could navigate better in the dark than he could by daylight.

Choosing a spot just out of sight of his neighbors, he built himself a house of stones and reeds. It consisted of two rooms, each about six by nine feet and a little over six feet high. Ever hopeful regarding the arrival of fresh recruits, Charles eventually constructed a "refectory" and "parlor" and a series of additional cells, each of the same claustrophobic dimensions. At the center of it all, when he was finished, was a burning lamp, indicating the presence of the Eucharist—to the eyes of faith, the very presence of Christ himself, here among the most abandoned and neglected. Charles spent hours each day prostrate before that lamp.

Meanwhile his letters, filled with chatty details of his daily life and spiritual reflections, were punctuated by the plaintive appeal: "My only regret is that I am still alone...Try to send me some brothers...I would so love to have a companion who would be my successor..." But this was not to be.

The years passed. Foucauld grew older. The plump young cadet was now a gaunt figure of middle age, bearded, almost bald, his skin darkened by the sun. His smile revealed missing teeth, while his eyes burned with a passionate intensity. From the time of his arrival in the Hoggar he had struggled hard to master the Tuareg language. The fruit of his study was recorded in a massive Tuareg dictionary, a manuscript completed shortly before his death and later found among his papers. Otherwise his was a life spent with little sign of outward accomplishment.

Nevertheless, as he wrote to a friend, "Living alone in the country is a good thing; one can act, even without doing much, because one becomes one of them. One is approachable, because one is so small." It was thus a fruitful loneliness, a way of being available to his neighbors. He had little to offer them but his friendship, his care, and occasional medicines. They had no use for his religion. But having overcome their initial suspicions of this strange foreigner who had traveled so far to share their poverty, Charles was accepted by the people of Tamanrasset. From there, by the ancient channels of Bedouin communication, his reputation extended throughout the Hoggar.

In 1908, after two years in Tamanrasset, Foucauld obtained a dispensation from the Vatican to say Mass by himself, without a server, as well as permission to construct a tabernacle for the reserved Eucharist. And so he was not entirely alone. "To receive the grace of God," he wrote to a Trappist, "you must go to a desert place and stay a while. There you can be emptied and un-burdened of everything that does not pertain to God. There the house of our soul is swept clean to make room for God alone to dwell...We need this silence, this absence of every creature, so that God can build his hermitage within us."

The spiritual path of Charles de Foucauld was modeled on the hidden life of Jesus in Nazareth, a way of constant abandon-ment to the love of God, whether in the silence of desert spaces or in the midst of others. There is no doubt that in embarking on this path Foucauld prepared himself to give everything and that he carefully calculated the cost. Already in 1897, while living in Nazareth, he had written in his journal:

> Think that you are going to die a martyr, stripped of everything, stretched out on the ground, naked, hardly recognizable, covered with blood and wounds, violently and painfully killed...and wish it to be today...think of this death often, prepare yourself for it and judge things at their true value.

IT WAS A REMARKABLY PROPHETIC MEDITATION. Was it also evidence of a morbid imagination? If so, it was a natural feature of a spirituality centered so closely on the imitation of Christ. "We cannot possibly love him without imitating him," he wrote. "Since he suffered and died in agony, we cannot love him and yet want to be crowned with roses while he was crowned with thorns...We must love him just as he loved us, in the very same way."

All the same, it seems that for Foucauld the consciousness of impending sacrifice grew over time to a steady conviction. Scattered throughout his journals one finds such statements as these: "To prepare oneself constantly for martyrdom, and accept it without a shadow of reluctance, like the divine Lamb, in Jesus, through Jesus, for Jesus." "I must try and live as if I were to die a martyr today. Every minute I must imagine I am going to be martyred this very evening." And in a booklet found on his body on the day he died: "My wish is to live as if I were to die a martyr today..."

Foucauld was granted this wish; so he lived, and so he died. And yet is it entirely accurate to describe Foucauld as a martyr? Among the motivations of those who killed him it is possible to discern a variety of factors beyond simple "hatred for the faith." But this is undoubtedly true with most martyrs, whose witness to Christ is inevitably complicated by cultural, ethnic, or political interests. As for Charles de Foucauld, it must be acknowledged that, despite his desire to live a hidden life as a brother to the Tuaregs, he was finally unable to obliterate his identity as a son of France and a former officer.

Foucauld deplored certain features of colonial rule, especially the failure of French authorities to check the ongoing commerce of slavery. But he continued to affirm an idealistic notion of France's role in bringing civilization and Christian morality to the benighted peoples of the Sahara. His criticism of colonial policy was that it failed to reflect its exalted purpose. As he wrote to a friend,

> I suffer as a Frenchman to see the natives not being ruled as they ought. On the contrary, the moral and spiritually

inadequate condition of these peoples is made all the worse by treating them as no more than a means of material acquisition. What the natives learn from the infidel Frenchmen who proclaim the doctrine of "fraternity" is neglect, or ambition, or greed, and from almost everyone, unfortunately, indifference, aversion and harsh behavior.

In another place he wrote, "If we act according to our lights, if we civilize instead of exploiting, in fifty years Algeria, Tunis and Morocco will be an extension of France. If we do not live up to our duty, if we exploit rather than civilize, we will lose everything and the union we have created from these diverse peoples will turn against us."

Throughout his years in North Africa Foucauld maintained friendly relations with the army. In a sense he had no other choice if he were to pursue his mission. But at the same time many of the officers were truly old friends from his earlier life. They consulted him about conditions in the interior, and he readily provided intelligence about the terrain, about the best locations for encampments, and about the dangers of bandits and rebels. The army in turn regarded him as a kind of French agent in the Hoggar. It was a role Charles did not positively decline.

The outbreak of World War I, which intensified conflicts between the army and rebel tribesmen, enhanced Charles's value to the colonial enterprise. Many of his army friends were recalled to the trenches in Europe, and Charles himself inquired about the chances of serving as a stretcher bearer. It was his old friend—now General—Laperrine who instructed him otherwise: "Stay in the Hoggar. We need you there." And so in his own corner of the world Charles was prepared to do his part.

In April 1916 a French stronghold at Djanet on the Libyan frontier fell to an army of Senoussi rebels. The Senoussi were a brotherhood of Muslim nationalists, drawn from a number of ethnic groups, united in their determination to drive the foreign infidels from the land of Islam. Warned that the Senoussi were drawing near to Tamanrasset, Charles decided to build a small

fortress. Using local materials over a period of months he managed to raise a formidable structure with walls a solid meter
thick. He finished the fortification on November 15. Visiting officers were impressed and asked his permission to store supplies
and weapons inside. Foucauld raised no objection.

It is difficult today to reconcile the image of Foucauld the
French patriot with the image of Charles, the Little Brother of
Jesus. By the same token, one can imagine with what ease the
Senoussi warriors who broke into his fort on December 1, who
bound his arms, shot him, and left him bleeding in the sand,
might confuse the holy Marabout for a representative of France.
For their careless violence they were rewarded with the contents
of his fort. Aside from supplies of food they recovered six cases
of ammunition and thirty carbines. They left his Tuareg dictionary scattered in the courtyard, along with the apparently worth-
less tabernacle, not to mention his body, all discovered later by
French troops. Such are the complexities of Charles de Foucauld
and the ambiguities of his death. By the end he had managed to
combine the heroic ideals of both his grandfather the colonel
and his pious mother, all reflected in the family motto: "Never
Retreat."

Foucauld himself was aware of the ironies of his existence.
Daily he confronted the weakness of his faith and the ambiguities
of his witness. In the end those ambiguities ran deeper than he
could acknowledge. But he prayed that if he made his small offering in love then God would purify his intentions and bring
forth the harvest from his small seeds. Ultimately, the meaning
of his life, distilled with the passage of time, had nothing to do
with carbines, forts, the honor of France, or even the matter of
his death. Instead, it rested on the spiritual vision he summarized
toward the end of his life:

> Jesus came to Nazareth, the place of the hidden life, of
> ordinary life, of family life, of prayer, work, obscurity,
> silent virtues, practiced with no witnesses other than
> God, his friends and neighbors. Nazareth, the place
> where most people lead their lives. We must infinitely re-

spect the least of our brothers... let us mingle with them. Let us be one of them to the extent that God wishes ... and treat them fraternally in order to have the honor and joy of being accepted as one of them.

Failing the joy of being accepted as one of them, there was another joy. On the last day of his life Charles wrote a letter to his cousin Marie, which was left sealed and ready for the mailman:

Our annihilation is the most powerful means that we have of uniting ourselves to Jesus. One finds one doesn't love enough, that is true, but Almighty God, who knows with what he has molded us, and who loves us much more than a mother can love her child, has said that he will not cast out those who come to him.

At that point he heard the knock on the door, the sound for which he had trained his ear: "Illness, danger, the prospect of death, it is the call. 'Here is the Spouse: go forth to meet him.'"

BY ANY CONVENTIONAL STANDARD, the life of Charles de Foucauld ended in failure. At the time of his violent death in a remote corner of the Sahara he had published none of his spiritual writings; he had founded no congregation nor attracted any followers. He could not even claim responsibility for a single conversion.

Ultimately, however, the reverberations from Foucauld's solitary witness would have considerable effect. In 1933, long after Foucauld's death, René Voillaume and four companions left France for the Sahara. Modeling themselves on Foucauld's example, they became the core of the Little Brothers of Jesus. A few years later they were joined by the Little Sisters of Jesus, founded by Madeline Hutin. Both fraternities, and their several offshoots, gradually spread throughout the world, their small communities taking up life among the poor and outcast, first in the Sahara desert, but eventually in many obscure corners of the globe.

And yet Foucauld's influence and challenge extend far beyond the numbers of his followers. His emphasis on the "hidden life" of Jesus bears implications for many aspects of Christian life today. For one thing, he anticipated a new model of contemplative life, not in a cloistered monastery but in the midst of the world. Thus he overcame the artificial divide between the "religious" and "secular" worlds, pointing to a way of holiness that is accessible to all of us, in whatever "desert" we may find ourselves.

Foucauld's approach to mission is particularly significant. In contrast to the triumphalistic models of his day, Foucauld exemplified what has come to be known as an evangelism of "presence," a willingness to encounter people of other faiths on a basis of equality and mutual respect. Although his asceticism was extreme by the standards of most missionaries or even of the Trappist monks with whom he lived for a time in Syria, he essentially embraced the poverty of his neighbors. He wanted to bear witness to the gospel by living it, by being a friend and brother to all. He knew how much the church undermines the credibility of its witness when its representatives enjoy a status and comfort far above the level of the poor.

Today as never before we are realizing the particular need for improved understanding between Christians and Muslims. Foucauld was himself killed by members of a Muslim sect whose fundamentalist zeal has obvious contemporary counterparts. And yet, if Foucauld's path had characterized the encounter between Christians and Muslims throughout history, who can say whether our relations today might be different? In an age when Christianity is no longer synonymous with the outreach of Western civilization and colonial power, the witness of Foucauld—poor, unarmed, stripped of everything, relying on no greater authority than the power of Love—may well represent the face of the future church, a church rooted in the memory of its origins and of its poor founder.

After a century exhausted by grand projects, world wars, and ostentatious display, Foucauld's appreciation for the value of inconspicuous means, modest goals, and the hidden life of faith and charity exerts a powerful and subversive challenge. It reminds us,

Charles de Foucauld in his final years

among other things, that Christ himself pursued the path of apparent failure, choosing "what is low and despised in the world, even things that are not, to bring to nothing things that are" (1 Cor 1:28).

I remember my first encounter with the spirituality of Charles de Foucauld, embodied by a small "fraternity" of the Little Brothers of the Gospel, one of the offshoots of his spiritual family. The Little Brothers, whose members hailed from Italy and France as well as a few from North America, shared a small apartment on the Lower East Side of New York, near the Catholic Worker. By day they worked in menial jobs, as janitors or in factories. Otherwise, they offered a loving witness of friendship to their poor neighbors—mostly Puerto Ricans, Dominicans, and African Americans. Their apartment was an oasis of prayer. One of their number, a former French "worker priest" named Peter, often said Mass at the Catholic Worker.

I remember a sermon that made a great impression on me, though in my memory it consisted of only one sentence: "In the gospels there are two kinds of people: there are the good people, and then there are the sinners that Jesus loved." I asked Fr. Peter if he would help me become a Catholic. And some months later, on Holy Thursday, in a small service in the chapel of the Little Brothers, I was received into the Catholic Church. Afterward Dorothy Day, who had herself maintained a great devotion to Foucauld, presented me with an old copy of René Bazin's biography of Brother Charles—the very book that had inspired René Voillaume to implement Foucauld's model of religious life. It was heavily underlined, and inside there was a photo of the desert hermit, on the back of which she had written: "Chas de Foucauld, pray for us all here at the CW—all who pass our portals, especially your followers."

Many today regard Foucauld as one of the great spiritual witnesses of the twentieth century, a prophet whose message speaks more clearly to the challenges of our time than it did to those of his own. With his beatification in 2005 the church at last extended official recognition to his significance as one of those seekers who, periodically, manage to reinvent the "imitation of Christ" in a manner suited to the needs of their age, and thus invite others to read the gospel in a new way.[1]

CHARLES DE FOUCAULD'S
"PRAYER OF ABANDONMENT"

Father,
I abandon myself into your hands;
do with me what you will.
Whatever you may do, I thank you:
I am ready for all, I accept all.

Let only your will be done in me,
and in all your creatures—
I wish no more than this, O Lord.

Into your hands I commend my soul:
I offer it to you with all the love of my heart,
for I love you, Lord, and so need to give myself,
to surrender myself into your hands without reserve,
and with boundless confidence,
for you are my Father.

8

HOLY WOMEN
Finding Their Own Path

SOON AFTER THE PUBLICATION OF MY BOOK *All Saints*, I received an invitation—perhaps summons is a better word—from the small community of cloistered Maryknoll Sisters across the street from my office. I expected they wished to thank me for having included their founder, Mother Mary Rogers, in my book. Instead, they made a pointed observation. They noted that, while *All Saints* departed significantly from traditional approaches to saints, in one respect it was quite traditional: namely, in maintaining the typical ratio of female to male saints, about one in four. Having pointed this out, the Sisters took the liberty of presenting me with a long list of suitable female candidates.

My first reaction was defensive; I didn't think I had gotten quite enough credit for including Mollie Rogers. But I had to concede their point. And this began a process of reflection that led, ultimately, to a second book, *Blessed Among All Women*. Continuing in that spirit, in my daily reflections on saints for *Give Us This Day* I have strived to maintain an equal balance of women and men.

No doubt there are numerous prominent women among the officially recognized or "canonized" saints of the church. Many

---

Originally delivered as a lecture, "Blessed Among All Women: The Subversive Power of Female Saints," at Duquesne University's Center for Women's and Gender Studies, March 26, 2015. Parts of this essay draw on my book, *Blessed Among All Women: Reflections on Women Saints, Prophets, and Witnesses for Our Time* (New York: Crossroad, 2007).

of them appeared in *All Saints*. That list begins with Mary, the mother of Jesus, whose consent to God's mysterious plan set in motion the subsequent history of salvation. First among the company of saints, she is addressed in prayer with the words originally spoken by her kinswoman Elizabeth: "Blessed are you among women, and blessed is the fruit of your womb."

Among those who followed, it would be easy to name figures like St. Monica, the mother of St. Augustine, who won her son's conversion through her tears; St. Brigid of Ireland, who pictured heaven as a giant lake of beer; and St. Clare of Assisi, the most faithful follower of St. Francis. There is St. Joan of Arc—who belongs in a category of her own, having been first burned as a heretic before her eventual canonization; and St. Teresa of Avila, reformer of the Carmelite order and a Doctor of the Church. She was once thrown from a donkey into a muddy river and heard a voice from heaven saying "This is how I treat my friends," evoking her tart reply, "Then it is no wonder you have so few of them." Among recent notable saints one could cite St. Edith Stein, the Jewish convert and Carmelite nun who died in Auschwitz; and of course Mother Teresa of Calcutta, one of the most popular saints of modern times.

And yet any consideration of women saints must begin with an unavoidable fact—that among the wide company of canonized saints, women are vastly underrepresented. A quick review of the classic English reference, *Butler's Lives of the Saints,* makes this abundantly clear.

This is a curious fact when we consider the prominent role of women in the ministry of Jesus—a fact to which all the gospels attest. Women appear there in a range of roles, whether as family members, friends, disciples, or strangers in need; Jesus is invariably at ease in their presence, always taking them seriously, never trivializing or patronizing them, never making jokes at their expense or telling them to stay in the kitchen. (On the contrary, when Martha asks Jesus to tell her sister to stop sitting at his feet and help in the kitchen, Jesus replies that Mary has chosen the better part.) Even in the case of women who are otherwise objects of social scorn—the poor, the sick and crazed, foreigners, the ritually "unclean," the notorious "sinner"—Jesus extends his care and attention, sometimes at the risk of provoking scandal. Because of this, many believe it fair to say that "Jesus was a feminist."

In contrast with the special attention accorded the Twelve (male) apostles, the prominence of women among Jesus' closest circle is often overlooked. And yet time and again it is women who are held up—by their exemplary faith or by doing the will of God—as paradigmatic disciples. Some of these women are named, particularly Mary Magdalene, the first to behold the risen Lord. All of the gospels agree that it was women such as these who remained faithful at the foot of the Cross and who later rushed to anoint Jesus' hastily buried body. The Gospel of Luke names Mary Magdalene, Joanna, and Mary the mother of James among those who returned from the empty tomb to report that Jesus was risen. When the "church" at that time had been effectively reduced to eleven frightened men cowering in an upper room, it was these women who were the first to proclaim the gospel. Yet when they tried to report this good news to the apostles, their testimony was dismissed: "These words seemed to them an idle tale, and they did not believe them."

But along with these named disciples and witnesses are many others whose names have been mysteriously effaced, including the Samaritan "woman at the well" who proclaimed the gospel to her neighbors. In contrast to the skepticism that greeted the women's report of the resurrection, it was said of this Samaritan woman that "many believed on the strength of her witness." There is the Syrophoenician mother who risked scorn on behalf of her sick child; the woman with "a flow of blood," who was healed as a result of her faith; the anonymous woman in Bethany who anointed Jesus with precious oil, inspiring Jesus' prediction that wherever the gospel would be repeated in the whole world her deed would be told "in memory of her." True enough. Her deed was remembered; even the names of the disciples who reproached her are remembered. But not her name.

Needless to say, the memory of these women did not translate into positions of leadership in the emerging church. In describing the spread of Christianity into the Gentile world, St. Paul

provides many glimpses of the important role of women, especially in the "house churches" that were the early cells of the
Christian community; a number of these women, like Lydia or
Prisca, are named in the Book of Acts or the Pauline epistles. But
already leadership and authority in the church were being
claimed and reserved for men. Women, in contrast, were enjoined
to "keep silent"; their wisdom, their voices, their very names were
being pushed to the margins.

This marginalization has continued in the area of official
recognition of women saints and female models of holiness. One
may speculate about the reasons for this. But lurking in the background is a basic fact: that the process of canonization, like the
general exercise of authority in the church, has been entirely con-
trolled by men. Women literally play no official role. This has affected not only the selection of saints for canonization but also
the interpretation of their lives.

Traditional accounts of women saints—almost always written
by men—have tended to emphasize "feminine virtues" of purity,
humble service, obedience, or patient endurance. Even the labels
attached to women saints reflect a narrow range of categories.

Apart from the martyrs, women saints are generally remembered as "virgins," "foundresses" of religious orders, widows, or
occasionally "matrons." It gives us the impression that the sanctity of women comes in a limited number of flavors, often determined by their marital status or sexual experience. (Even nuns
are traditionally counted as "brides of Christ," a status not assigned to male members of religious orders.)

Needless to say, such labels elide the range of functions such
women may have performed, whether as theologians, prophets,
healers, visionaries, or trailblazers in the spiritual life. The
process of canonization often excels in conforming saints to a
stereotypical mold. The first thing we ought to do is break
through these molds and to see instead how holy women also
questioned authority, defied restrictive codes and models of behavior, displayed audacity and wit in surmounting the obstacles
placed in their paths. Long after their deaths, reformers and

prophets like St. Teresa of Avila, St. Catherine of Siena, St. Hildegard of Bingen, St. Birgitta of Sweden, and St. Joan of Arc were honored—with little acknowledgment that while they lived they were considered insufferable troublemakers, and with no pondering the implications and lessons this might hold for our present day. In effect we need to take such saints down from their pedestals—not just for the sake of respecting the truth of their lives, but so that we can liberate their message and uphold their challenge for our own time.

THE SHAPING OF THE MEMORY of holy women began with the earliest female saints of the church. These are the so-called Virgin Martyrs—women like Sts. Catherine of Alexandria, Agnes, Cecilia, Barbara, Dorothy, and many others. By and large their stories follow a standard pattern: a Christian woman living during a time of Roman persecution cites her espousal to Christ as the reason for her refusal to marry or worship idols. In retaliation she is typically subjected to hideous tortures, often with sado-sexual overtones. Her resistance is taken not just as an affront to the Roman gods but as an attack on the very order of patriarchy itself.

These women have traditionally been held up as paragons of sexual purity. But when we read their stories through a gospel lens I think we discover a different motif, one that connects them with a line of holy women that extends to our own time. The opposition in these stories is not between sex and holiness. Rather, it lies in a conflict between a young woman's power in Christ to define her own identity versus a patriarchal culture's claim to define her identity in terms of gender or sexuality. These women refused to worship the gods of their culture. The God they worshiped set an altogether different value on their bodies, their identities, and their human worth.

The power of such liberated women is prominently highlighted in one of the most poignant documents of the early church, "The Passion of Sts. Perpetua and Felicity." This text recounts the martyrdom of Perpetua, a prosperous young woman of second-century Carthage, who, at the age of twenty-two was arrested along with her servant Felicity for violating a prohibition against conversion to Christianity. The narrative, most of which purports to represent the actual voice of Perpetua, is a uniquely personal document, filled with intimate details, describing her hunger, fears, and even—as a nursing mother separated from her child—the pain of swollen breasts.

While the overall plot focuses on Perpetua's approaching passion, she is called throughout to negotiate a series of complications arising from her status as a woman—daughter, mother, spouse. The same holds for Felicity, who is eight months pregnant at the time of her ordeal. Throughout we sense the struggle of two women to claim their own identities and vocation amidst the various competing claims imposed by society. Even at their trial the proconsul appeals to Perpetua's sense of duty toward her aged father and her infant son. Perpetua answers the court with a simple declaration: "I am a Christian." One senses that in Christ she has found the power and freedom to name herself and the courage to accept the consequences.

And yet there is no suggestion that Perpetua scorns motherhood or the bonds of family. The narrative describes in touching detail the suffering caused by her separation from her infant son. But when he is restored to her and she is able to nurse him, "straightway I became well and was lightened of my labor and care for the child; and suddenly the prison was made a palace for me, so that I would sooner be here than anywhere else."

Her servant Felicity feared that because of her advanced pregnancy she would be separated from her companions. But after a night of ardent prayer, she goes into labor and gives birth to a daughter, whom she is able to entrust, along with Perpetua's son, to Christian friends.

On their last day the prisoners are marched from the darkness of their prison into the glaring amphitheater, "as it were to heaven, cheerful and bright of countenance." Perpetua wears the expression of a "true spouse of Christ," while Felicity, rejoicing that her child was born in safety, "came now from blood to blood, from the midwife to the gladiator, to wash after her labor in a second baptism."

In the arena together the two women are stripped, causing the crowd to shudder, "seeing one a tender girl, the other her breasts yet dropping from her late childbearing." After they have been tossed by a wild cow, the executioner is ordered to put them to the sword. But the swordsman is apparently a novice, and has trouble striking a true blow. The narrator relates that Perpetua, in the final mark of her mastery over her fate, directed the blow to her own neck: "Perhaps so great a woman could not else have been slain had she not herself so willed it." There is a final poignant image. The narrator also notes that before meeting the sword the two young women, formerly mistress and servant, now sisters in Christ, turned to one another before the jeering crowd and exchanged a kiss.

"The Passion of Sts. Perpetua and Felicity"—a text, we are told, that competed for popularity in the North African Church with the gospels themselves—is unusual among the accounts of female martyrs in that the defense of virginity is not a factor. (In the more typical story of St. Agnes, a thirteen-year-old girl who proclaimed her espousal to Christ, the magistrate first consigns her to a brothel, where every man might have free use of her. It is found, however, that she exudes such a powerful aura of purity that no one can lay a finger on her.) Even in modern times, the accounts of women martyrs, like the child Maria Goretti, who died in 1902, often emphasize their witness to sexual purity. Maria and her poor family were forced to live with another family. When Maria was not yet twelve, she resisted the advances of an older son of the host family, who tried to rape her. "No, it's a sin, God doesn't want it," she cried out, before being stabbed. She died the next day, after having forgiven her assailant. In addressing the enormous crowd that witnessed her canonization in 1950, Pope Pius XII emphasized her role as a martyr for sexual morality, and called on young girls to heed her message.

But what was that message? If Maria had survived her rape and then expressed the same astonishing charity toward her assailant, would she have been similarly honored by her family and the church? In a similar spirit, the church recently beatified a young Slovak woman, Anna Kolesarova, who was killed in 1944 by a Russian soldier who was attempting to rape her. She was fifteen. Pope Francis said she was "killed for having resisted one who wanted to violate her dignity and chastity." In this case there was no edifying story of forgiveness toward the assailant (who in Maria Goretti's case survived to attend the young martyr's canonization). Nevertheless, the pope said, "She is like our Italian Maria Goretti. May this courageous girl help Christian young people to remain firm in fidelity to the Gospel, also when it requires going against the current and paying personally." *Going against the current?*

Dorothy Day, writing in the earliest account of her conversion, devotes an entire chapter to her best friend in college, a young woman named Rayna Prohme—an atheist who in fact later became a communist but who made a tremendous impression on all who encountered her, Day in particular. Reflecting on her example, Day writes, "Most young people think of virtue as something negative. They think that by avoiding sin they are being good. They think of purity as an absence of impurity. They have not committed those sins which they might have committed. Yet we should think certainly of purity as a shining positive virtue, rather than as a negative one." She continues: "Have you not met in your life people who stood out because some virtue shone in them, was predominant? I can remember people whose goodness shone as a positive adornment, which attracted others and filled them with longing . . . Rayna's truth stood out as a positive virtue. She was honest, pure, loving, but above all shone her joyousness and her truth."[1] It is this positive spiritual power that, in so many accounts of women saints, is somehow tamed or conformed to fit stereotypical standards of purity or virtue.

In 1981 Salvadoran troops occupied the town of El Mozote in a province largely under guerrilla control. Over a period of days the soldiers gathered all the residents—as many as one thousand men, women, and children—and massacred them all. One woman, Rufina Amaya, managed to survive by hiding in some bushes. She had to listen to the sounds of her own children being killed, biting her tongue to keep from screaming. That night she heard some of the soldiers discussing the faith of the people they had killed. One young girl in particular remained on their minds. While they had raped her repeatedly, she had continued to sing hymns. Even after they shot her in the chest, she sang. They shot her again, and still she sang. And then "their wonder began to turn to fear—until finally they had unsheathed their machetes and hacked through her neck, and at last the singing stopped."[2]

The Passion of Sts. Perpetua and Felicity is unusual for its realism and historical color. But along with the stories of other "virgin martyrs" and contemporary witnesses like St. Maria Goretti, it is marked by qualities of agency, freedom, and self-determination that are seldom emphasized in traditional accounts of women saints. It is a positive quality, a subversive power that has nothing to do with virtue or morality in the conventional sense. In the case of the unnamed martyr of El Mozote, or the four North American churchwomen who were raped before being killed by Salvadoran soldiers in 1980, it is an aura of purity that is beyond the power of any tormentor to violate.

IN THE CASE OF MOST HOLY WOMEN, the affirmation of their personal truth does not entail the actual laying down of their lives. Most of them have been, as George Eliot described her heroine in *Middlemarch,* "foundresses of nothing," their lives poured out in "unhistoric acts" of service, hospitality, and devotion. Yet it is striking, in reading the lives of women saints, how frequently we discover the common theme—especially among women who felt stultified by their privileged station—of a desire to *do* more, to *be more,* to rise to some higher cause or purpose. There is St. Catherine of Genoa (d. 1510) who escaped the depression induced by her unhappy marriage by volunteering at the local hospital, and who went on to become not only the hospital administrator but one of the great mystics of the church. Or Rose Hawthorne, daughter of the famous novelist Nathaniel Hawthorne, who took to nursing homeless cancer patients in

New York before starting her own branch of the Dominican Order. In so many cases women responded to the needs at hand: there were orphans to be cared for; sick people to be nursed; young women abandoned to prostitution; children who needed an education; workers with no one to attend to their spiritual needs. Religious life often offered the best means of pursuing this dedicated service, without the encumbrance of family responsibilities. But even then, it was often a struggle to find authorization, support, or even freedom from interference.

THE HISTORY OF CHRISTIANITY is marked by the stories of countless holy women who struggled hard to assert their full humanity and to follow where God was calling them, even when this challenged the prevailing options of their time—even when this truly meant "going against the current and paying personally." The same may be said of many male saints. But in the case of women saints, this often meant something extra and more specific: challenging the assigned gender codes of their culture—in some cases codes invested with divine authority—in order to assert their own spiritual integrity.

For some, this meant claiming the freedom to remain unmarried; for others, to escape the restrictive enclosure of a convent, to engage in active apostolic work among the poor, or to travel across the world to proclaim the gospel. Some claimed the authority to write their own community rules, to interpret scripture in new ways, or simply to describe their own experience of God. Others found in Christ a mandate to oppose slavery, war, and social injustice. Later, in light of their achievements and the space they created for new models of discipleship, such women were sometimes honored as "faithful daughters of the church." But while they lived they often endured extraordinary opposition or even persecution. In the struggle to pursue their vocations—especially if this involved any form of innovation—holy women have typically contended with male authorities who were only too eager to inform them that their visions or desires contradicted the will of God.

Mary Ward

CONSIDER THE STORY OF MARY WARD, founder of the Institute of the Blessed Virgin Mary, who died in 1645.[3] Her life was set against the background of Elizabethan England and intense persecution of the Catholic religion. Her family was among the landed gentry whose wealth and title allowed some private space to resist the severe anti-Catholic decrees. Her childhood was marked by secret visits from priests—often Jesuits— who had been quickly ordained overseas, smuggled into the country, and secretly passed from house to house to celebrate their forbidden Masses. This illicit practice of the Catholic religion was an act of treason, which could mean death not only for the priest but also for the sheltering family. In this context, Mary insisted that she was called to be a nun—a somewhat fantastic notion, given that at the time there was not a single remaining convent in England. Nevertheless, with the grudging support of her confessor, she won her family's approval and so was smuggled out of the country to Catholic Belgium.

Unfortunately, Mary had difficulty finding the vocation she was seeking. She had come to believe that she was not called to conventional enclosed religious life. Instead, inspired by the example of the Jesuits, she conceived of an institute of women living in a non-enclosed community, free of episcopal authority, who could carry out apostolic work in the world. To say the least, it was an idea ahead of its times.

Nevertheless, Mary was able to convince a number of influential church authorities, including a good Jesuit confessor, of the value of her plan. There followed the first of a number of clandestine visits to England to seek recruits for her community. Disguised as a traveling gentlewoman, she made the rounds of Catholic households, exhorting the faithful, helping to prepare people for baptism, visiting and comforting imprisoned priests, and inspiring a half dozen women to take the leap with her into the unknown.

During one of these visits she was finally discovered and imprisoned. Sentenced to death, she was instead permitted to accept exile. Back on the Continent, Mary went about forming her band of followers into a religious community while simultaneously pursuing official approval for her Institute. In Rome, she won an audience with the pope, who tentatively permitted her to develop her project. But formal recognition was not forthcoming.

Her enemies, as she discovered, were not only in Protestant England. Her devotion to the spiritual vision of St. Ignatius fed the distrust of secular clergy, who were rivals of the glamorous Society of Jesus. Her Institute was mocked as a house of "Lady Jesuits." But beyond the territorial jealousies of English Catholics, there was the wider resistance, in principle, to her radical vision. Her adamant insistence that the Institute be non-enclosed and remain free of episcopal governance ran head-on against the prescribed place of women in the church. While some bishops offered polite approval for her plans, especially her schools for girls, most ultimately shared the opinion of one priest who noted, "When all is said and done they are but women!"

After she had established a number of houses and won wide admiration for her exemplary schools, notification came from Rome in January 1631 that the Institute was to be suppressed. Within days, messengers arrived to take Mary into custody on the charge of being a "heretic, schismatic, and rebel to the Holy Church." Though her imprisonment in a convent was brief, the suppression of the Institute continued in effect, and she remained under a cloud of ecclesial disapprobation. In broken health she returned to England, where the penal laws against Catholics were still in effect, and where once again she faced surveillance and the possibility of arrest. She died in York at the age of sixty. Official recognition of her Institute would come only fifty-eight years after her death.

THE LAST TWO CENTURIES have been marked by dramatic and accelerating changes in the role and status of women in the church and society. The struggle by women to assert their equality and to challenge patriarchal structures and values has been one of the true signs of the times. In this struggle, it is probably safe to say that more dramatic changes in consciousness and social custom have occurred in the past fifty years than in many preceding centuries.

Catholic women have not always served in the forefront of these movements for change. Nevertheless, the history of female holiness, from the anonymous disciples of the New Testament up to the present, could be told as a story of women who discovered, through their relationship with Christ, the power to name themselves, to express their identity, and to value their own experience in ways that often set them apart from the roles defined by the church or the wider culture of their time.

Many of the great women saints of history are certainly in this category. There is St. Hildegard of Bingen, an eleventh-century abbess and mystic, who was clearly one of the remarkable figures of her age: founder of a Benedictine religious community; author and theologian; prophet and preacher; musician and composer of works that are still performed; poet and artist; doctor and pharmacist who anticipated the principles of homeopathy.[4] Yet for eight hundred years she remained in relative obscurity. Only in recent decades has she emerged into the light, partly thanks to contemporary interest in the role of women in history— yet also in belated recogni-

St. Hildegard of Bingen

tion of an ecologically minded and holistic spirituality that speaks prophetically to our own time.

Hildegard had a wide understanding of the cosmos as a whole and of the human place in it. Human beings, she wrote, are the universe in microcosm—made of the same elements that constitute the world. But within the great cosmos human beings are the thinking heart, called to be co-creators with God in shaping the world. Through human sin the world fell out of harmony with the Creator. But this did not erase the original goodness and blessing of creation. Through Christ—first fruits of a new creation—the cosmos and human beings find their way back to their original destiny. Constantly Hildegard refers to God as "Living Light," and employs a remarkable word—"greenness"—to describe the animating energy or grace of God that shines forth in all living things. For this wide-ranging and holistic vision she was recently named by Pope Benedict XVI as a Doctor of the Church. And yet this proclamation fails to acknowledge or reflect on the irony that until that point Hildegard had not been officially canonized; that in fact she was excommunicated in the last years of her life, her convent placed under interdict, and her teachings essentially ignored for many centuries.

LEST WE SUPPOSE THAT SUCH ORDEALS are a relic of the dark ages, I was struck in reflecting on women saints in the nineteenth century by how often their lives were marked—almost as a rite of passage—by actual periods of excommunication. This is seldom emphasized in their official vitae, which again tend to emphasize traditional virtues of piety, submission, and obedience.

Consider, for example, one of the recently canonized saints of the Americas, Mother Theodore Guerin (1798–1856), founder of the Sisters of Providence of St. Mary of the Woods.[5] She is remembered for her work in bringing a community of sisters from France to a new mission in the frontier territory of Indiana. Beginning with their foundation in a log cabin in the middle of the forest, the sisters contended with fierce winters, fires, locusts, droughts, and floods, while they steadily developed their ministry among the pioneer settlers of the region. And yet, again, the most difficult ordeal of their early years involved relations with their local bishop. Mother Theodore initially described him as "an excellent father." Never, she said, had she found "a heart more compassionate under an exterior so cold." But before long she was describing

Mother Theodore Guerin

his temperament as "one of those which makes martyrs of their possessors and still more of those who must put up with them."

The problem, it seems, was that the bishop regarded the community as his personal possession, and he sought to control and manage its affairs in every detail. "I have the greatest aversion to this kind of administration," Mother Theodore wrote. "It seems to me it would keep the sisters in a species of slavery."

The bishop tried to revise the sisters' rule. He tried to force the community to depose Mother Theodore as their superior. He insisted that neither she nor any other Sister leave the diocese without his written permission. Claiming that the land under their home was his, he announced, "I am the proprietor, spiritual and temporal, of that house."

When Mother Theodore resisted this interference, the bishop announced that she was no longer a Sister of Providence—he had released her from her vows. He ordered her to leave the diocese and "go elsewhere to hide her disgrace." When her Sisters vowed to follow her, he threatened to have them all excommunicated, and even to have them pursued by the law.

Fortunately, this story had a happy ending. Just as things were reaching a crisis, word came that the Vatican had accepted the retirement of the bishop in question and that his replacement was on his way. Under the new bishop's benevolent protection the congregation flourished, and a hundred and fifty years later Mother Theodore was recognized as a saint.

Yet the happy ending of this story stands in contrast with other oft-repeated stories of holy foundresses whose congregations were essentially usurped by priests or bishops, who were consigned to menial tasks in their communities, whose names were erased from the histories of the congregations they had founded, only to be restored long after their deaths.

AND YET IN OUR OWN TIME, no less than in the past, bold female leadership in the religious realm makes church authorities nervous. This was clearly demonstrated in the investigation over several recent years of the Leadership Conference of Women Religious, a canonical organization that represents 80 percent of women religious in the United States.[6] Several years ago, the LCWR received a notification from the Congregation for the Doctrine of the Faith accusing the organization of promoting an agenda of radical feminism and of focusing too much on the poor and issues of social justice at the expense of the right-to-life agenda and the "biblical view of the family." This was begun prior to the election of Pope Francis, and in fact, with his support, the investigation was abruptly and, apparently happily, concluded.

But that doesn't entirely erase the larger point. No group within the church has struggled more faithfully than women religious to heed the challenge of Vatican II, to examine their vocations and revise their forms of life to adapt to the needs of the gospel in our time. They have relinquished property and power and have increasingly aligned themselves with the poorest and the most marginalized members of society, and in so doing have tended to the wounds of Christ. They have taken on that "smell of the sheep" that Pope Francis has said should characterize true shepherds in the church. In a very special way these women religious have modeled the prophetic, self-giving, and self-emptying love of Jesus in our world.

The disciples were scandalized by Jesus' familiarity and his level of comfort around such women. The male disciples did not like to see women lavish affection on him, or touch him, or sit at his feet to receive his teaching. Yet it was women such as these who fed him, welcomed him in their homes, washed his tired feet, risked their lives to accompany him to the cross, who gathered at his tomb to perform the duties of burial, and who were the first to announce the good news that Jesus was risen.

I believe the women religious who have been criticized, who have been told they cannot be trusted to set their own agendas or organize their own meetings without episcopal oversight, are in a long line of holy women in the church. And whatever else one can say of their critics, and their intentions or motives, I believe they too are in a long line of male authorities who have taken it upon themselves to lecture women on the subject of their proper place. For them Jesus had words. As he said to the disciples who reproved the anonymous anointer of Bethany: "Leave her alone."

WHAT IN THE END are some of the conclusions to be drawn from the chronicles of women saints, whether canonized or not?

There are of course as many types of saints as there are people. Each one offers a unique glimpse of the face of God, each enlarges our moral imagination; each offers new insights into the meaning and possibilities of human life. To the extent that women's names have been forgotten, their stories left untold, their dreams, visions, and wisdom marginalized, these possibilities remain unknown and unfulfilled. We suffer the same loss when women's experience and examples are conformed to restrictive and stereotypical preconceptions of holiness.

But to hold up these lives is not just a matter of providing equal time. Because of the restrictions and obstacles they have overcome or transcended in a fundamentally patriarchal church and culture, I find the example of women saints particularly compelling and inspiring. They dramatize in a special way the challenge we all face to discern our own way to holiness, apart from the well-worn paths of the past or the conventional wisdom of the present. So many women saints could share the motto applied to St. Angela Merici, founder of the Ursuline order: "A Woman Faced with Two Alternatives, She Saw and Chose the Third." More than ever before, we are in need of such models of creativity and originality.

I LOOK BACK WITH GRATITUDE to the Maryknoll Sisters who encouraged me to explore these stories. In their honor, let me give the last word to the story of their founder, Mollie Rogers, an example of that creativity and originality, who died in 1950.[7]

Rogers dated the beginning of her vocation to a summer evening at Smith College when a crowd of her fellow students rushed outdoors singing "Onward Christian Soldiers." They had just signed the Student Volunteer pledge to go to China as Protestant missionaries. Mollie regretted that there was no similar Catholic mission group she could support. Making her way to the parish church, she offered a prayer, and "measured my faith and the expression of it by the sight I had just witnessed."

Years passed. Eventually she became one of a small group of women who volunteered to join the priests in New York who were launching the mission society that would become known as Maryknoll. At first, they were confined to secretarial work. But eventually Mollie asked why there should not be a mission order for women, serving not simply as auxiliaries to the priests, but engaging in overseas mission work.

This plan encountered resistance from Vatican officials who doubted that women were suited to the rugged demands of mission. Furthermore, the congregation Rogers envisioned represented a departure from the conventional model of religious life. She wished the Sisters to live amid the people—not cooped up in monastic enclosures, but able to move about and bear witness to the gospel. Despite reservations, the Vatican in 1920 granted approval. A year later Mollie and twenty-one other women made their formal religious vows as Maryknoll Sisters. She became Mother Mary Joseph.

They were assisted in their early formation by members of other religious congregations. But Rogers found it difficult to adjust to the discipline and spirituality of these nuns, rooted as they were in the traditions of the old world. Refusing "to be hampered by an over-regimented and parceled-out prayer life," she fought hard to impress on her congregation the importance of flexibility and individuality. Describing the ideal Maryknoll Sister (in words that might well apply to the ideal Christian, whether male or female), she said, "I would have her distinguished by Christ-like charity, a limpid simplicity of soul, heroic generosity, selflessness, unfailing loyalty, prudent zeal, gracious courtesy, an adaptable disposition, solid piety, and the saving grace of a kindly humor."

Mother Mary Joseph

These qualities are evident in my favorite photograph of Mother Mary Joseph—taken toward the end of her life. She is in motion, her large figure ensconced in a flowing black habit, her gaze at the camera capturing an expression of joy, energy, and determination, as if the life of faith were the greatest possible adventure.

A JOURNEY FAITH

JUST A FEW MONTHS following his election in 2013, Pope Francis granted an extraordinary interview to the Jesuit press.[1] There he shared his views on the church ("a field hospital"); the confessional ("not a torture chamber"); his favorite saint (Jesuit Peter Faber); his love of opera, the films of Fellini, and the art of Chagall; and his "dogmatic certainty": that "God is in every person's life."

Among the points that received less attention, though it offers a key to the pope's thinking on many subjects, was his distinction between what he called a "lab [or laboratory] faith" and a "journey faith": "There is always the lurking danger of living in a laboratory. Ours is not a lab faith, but a journey faith, a historical faith. God has revealed himself as history, not as a compendium of abstract truths..."[2]

In a "lab faith" everything is certain and mathematical; the greatest threats come from relativism, doubt, and uncertainty. But such a faith can be inflexible—ill prepared to deal with the messiness of life or the nature of reality. Presuming to know all the answers in advance, a lab faith may leave us impervious to the surprising promptings of the Holy Spirit.

Francis gives a concrete example: When he was twenty-one he had a life-threatening lung infection. While he was in the hospital his life was saved by the quick thinking of a nurse. "The doctor, who really was a good one, lived in his laboratory; the [nurse] lived on the frontier and was in dialogue with it every day...Laboratories are useful, but reflection for us must always start from experience."[3]

In contrast to a "lab faith," a "journey faith" is at home on the frontier. Starting with experience rather than with abstract

Pope Francis when he was archbishop of Buenos Aires

truths, it is constantly open to uncertainty and risk. If a "lab faith" prizes certainty, a journey faith values trust, patience, a capacity to endure or even embrace uncertainty. This is where the Ignatian principle of "discernment"— which is really about how to make one's way and form decisions in the face of uncertainty—comes in. Such discernment, the pope says, "redeems the necessary ambiguity of life and helps us find the most appropriate means, which do not always coincide with what looks great and strong."[4]

A journey faith is best described in terms of narrative. Describing the vocation of a Jesuit, Pope Francis says, "The Society of Jesus can be described only in narrative form. Only in narrative form do you discern, not in a philosophical or theological explanation . . . The Jesuit must be a person whose thought is incomplete, in the sense of open-ended . . . And that pushes the Society to be searching, creative, and generous."[5]

Clearly, what Pope Francis describes as a Jesuit trait also points to his ideal for all Christians. In a journey faith there is much that is unknown: the "truth" emerges through experience, through context, through relationships. A journey faith implies the capacity for change or conversion, the capacity to discover new and unfamiliar truths.

IN AMERICAN LITERATURE one of the best depictions of such a "journey faith" can be found in Mark Twain's *Huckleberry Finn*. Set in an actual journey, it tells the story of Huck, a young boy on the run from an abusive father and a world of corruption and hypocrisy, and of his relationship with Jim, a runaway slave with whom he shares a raft on the Mississippi River. In principle, Huck accepts the moral code of his slave-owning society—a morality supported by a certain (false) version of Christianity. According to this code it is not just a crime but a sin to assist in the escape of a slave. Insofar as he is doing just that, Huck experiences shame and remorse, and fears that he is bound for hell. But at a certain point he comes to recognize Jim as a fellow human being—a friend who inspires trust, loyalty, and even love. In the course of his journey he becomes open to a different kind of truth.

The moral climax of the novel comes when Huck is preparing to cleanse his soul by writing a letter to Jim's owner, telling her where to find her slave. But then he "got to thinking about our trip down the river; and see Jim before me all the time; in the day, and in the night-time, sometimes moonlight, sometimes storms, and we a-floating along, talking, and singing, and laughing." He remembers Jim's kindness and tenderness toward him, how he would "always call me honey, and pet me, and do everything he could think of for me, and how good he always was." And then he considers the letter in his hand. "I was a-trembling because I'd got to decide forever, betwixt two things, and I knowed it. I studied it a minute, sort of holding my breath, and then says to myself: 'All right then, I'll *go* to hell'—and tore it up."

Huck has discovered a higher truth than the morality of his society, a "Christian" ethic that justifies owning other human beings and offers a $200 reward for their return. Through discernment, he has discovered what it means, as the pope says, to have "a big heart open to God and to others."

In a journey faith, we don't know all the answers in advance. We have to pray, to reflect, to listen to how God is speaking to us through the events of history or the circumstances of our own life. As Pope Francis notes, "Our life is not given to us like an opera libretto, in which all is written down; but it means going, walking, doing, searching, seeing...We must enter into the adventure of the quest for meeting God; we must let God search and encounter us...God is encountered walking along the path."[6]

Franz Jägerstätter

The story of Franz Jägerstätter, the sole Catholic layman executed in Austria for refusing to serve in Hitler's army, is a study in that quest for meeting God along the path. In his youth, Franz had earned a reputation for rowdiness. After his marriage to his wife Francizka, however, neighbors observed a growing seriousness about his faith. He and his wife had two children, and he adopted another child he had previously fathered out of wedlock. He became a Third Order Franciscan and served as a sexton in his local parish. But how did this farmer, alone in his village, and evidently in his whole country, come to see so clearly that any compromise with the Nazi system—which he believed was a satanic movement—would imperil his immortal soul? In an account of his thinking, written in prison at the request of a chaplain, he described a dream he had had soon after the Anschluss, a plebiscite that authorized the incorporation of Austria into Greater Germany. Franz wrote that in his dream he saw a great shiny train, one which crowds of people—important people, even priests and bishops—were clamoring to board. When he asked the conductor where this train was headed, the answer was, "This train is bound for hell." On waking he determined that the train represented National Socialism, carrying the whole country to destruction. Surely, he thought, one should jump off such a train, once one knows its destination.

Still, as he faced the question of whether to cooperate with conscription, which would entail an oath of allegiance to the Fuhrer, he thought he should seek pastoral advice. He went first to his local priest and then even traveled to consult with his bishop. They both advised him that such political questions were not his responsibility; his primary duty was to his Fatherland,

and to his family. As for the larger moral issues, he should leave those in God's hands. Of course, the bishop who offered this advice was not exceptional; it is doubtful that any bishop in the world at that time would have counseled Franz otherwise. Nevertheless, he could not be persuaded by these arguments. In the gospel he had found a higher truth that contradicted the morality of his society and his church. He did not find his answers in a laboratory, but through discernment, through the challenges of history, as he attempted to walk the path of discipleship.

Franz's witness has a counterpart in the faith and love of his wife Franziska. Though her deep piety had played a significant role in shaping Franz's exacting conscience, she naturally wished that Franz might find some compromise that would spare his life and allow him to return to his family. But once his mind was set, she did not try to deflect him, despite the urging of her priest and the prison chaplain. After learning of his death, she wrote, "I have lost a good husband and exemplary father for my children ... However, the loving God had ordained things to be otherwise, and our beautiful union was lost. I already look forward to our reunion in heaven where no war can any longer separate us." Franziska Jägerstätter was alive in 2007 to attend her husband's beatification.

Franz acted without any expectation that his stance would bring down the Third Reich—or that anyone would even know of or remember his sacrifice. In fact he remained largely unknown to the world until an American Catholic scholar, Gordon Zahn—himself a former conscientious objector—recounted his story in his book *In Solitary Witness*.[7] That book was one of the things that influenced my father's decision to copy and release the Pentagon Papers—an action that resulted in his being charged with crimes that carried a maximum penalty of 115 years in prison. He in turn passed that book along to me.

I was fifteen when I was called to testify before a grand jury investigating my father's copying of the Pentagon Papers. I was seventeen in 1973 when the charges against him were dismissed on the grounds of gross governmental misconduct. Nevertheless, the Vietnam War continued. For years I had anticipated my own appointment with destiny—not in the indeterminate future, but on the date when I would turn eighteen and face the legal obligation of registering for the draft. Thoughts of Franz Jägerstätter played in my mind. I thought in particular about Franz's dream about the train, and his warning that we must surely jump off that train, or refuse to climb on board, when we know its destination. I decided that, rather than apply for conscientious objector status when the time came, I would refuse to register at all.

I turned eighteen that December, during my freshman year in college. By that time the draft had ended—a wrinkle in my plan, to be sure, though it didn't cause me to reconsider. On my birthday I wrote a very heroic letter to the Selective Service System, informing them of my resistance. And then I forgot all about it. A couple of months passed before I received a very official-looking letter informing me that I had sixty days to register before my case would be turned over to the Justice Department for "prosecutive determination"; my offense carried a penalty of five years in prison. I read the letter several times before noticing a curious fact, that the date on the letter was already more than sixty days old. I looked out the window, half expecting a knock on the door. Suddenly, the import of my gesture became very real.

For several months I thought of almost nothing else but "The Problem" (in my mind it was always capitalized). This was quite boring to my friends, but I felt fantastically alive. Everything took on a new significance; every day seemed to disclose some special message, often in the form of dictums that were tacked to my consciousness, such as: Beware of Doing the Right Thing for the Wrong Reasons. Among my classmates I didn't know anyone who comprehended why I was obsessing about all this; after all, the draft had ended, the war was winding down. Was I truly prepared to go to prison for this? The answer, eventually, was no. I grew exhausted by The Problem. I didn't have the resources to follow through on my brave resolution. That spring I took a bus to the Selective Service office and signed their forms. I made sure to tell the clerk I was doing this *under protest,* though she displayed no interest, one way or the other.

So that was the end of that. But not really. I had an idea of what I was *against.* But what was my life *for?* I wasn't sure there was a correct answer to my dilemma. I was not familiar with the practice of "discernment," but it felt as if there were questions in life that were worth troubling over. The following year I dropped out of college and made my way to the Catholic Worker—drawn, not by anything to do with Catholicism, to be sure, but by a sense that this was a community of moral purpose, a place where my questions and problems (lower-cased) wouldn't seem quite so eccentric. That expectation was fulfilled—along with other things beyond my capacity, at that time, to expect.

A JOURNEY FAITH—like any journey—begins with the first steps. Perhaps we don't even realize, at the time, that it has begun. Certainly we have no idea where it will end. Its entire character is defined by uncertainty, which calls for the exercise of trust, faith, and hope. In the case of so many saints—at least the ones who particularly interest me—those qualities had to substitute for maps. Thomas Merton made this clear in a famous prayer:

> My Lord God, I have no idea where I am going. I do not see the road ahead of me. I cannot know for certain where it will end. Nor do I really know myself, and the fact that I think I am following your will does not mean that I am actually doing so. But I believe that the desire to please you does in fact please you. And I hope I have that desire in all that I am doing. I hope that I will never do anything apart from that desire. And I know that if I do this you will lead me by the right road, though I may know nothing about it. Therefore I will trust you always though I may seem to be lost and in the shadow of death. I will not fear, for you are ever with me and you will never leave me to face my perils alone.[8]

A similar attitude is reflected in a prayer that Henri Nouwen wrote four months before his death:

> I do not know where you will lead me. I do not know where I will be two, five, or ten years from now. I do not know the road ahead of me, but I know now that you are with me to guide me and that, wherever you lead me, even where I would rather not go, you will bring me closer to my true home. Thank you, Lord, for my life, for my vocation, and for the hope that you have planted in my heart. Amen.[9]

It was that hope, planted in the hearts of the saints, rather than any handbook or manual of instructions, that was their compass, leading them to their true home. And it was on that path that they encountered God.

I think of Dorothy Day at the time of her conversion, sacrificing everything that she held most dear, stepping into an unknown future. She spent five lonely years in the wilderness, searching for her vocation. On the feast of the Immaculate Conception in 1932 she prayed that she might find some way of connecting her faith and her commitment to the cause of the poor, the oppressed. There was no obvious model at hand, even among the saints she revered. She had to invent her own way. Five months later, with Peter Maurin, she launched the Catholic Worker movement.

Many years later, at a Quaker retreat center in Pennsylvania, Dorothy happened to meet Fritz Eichenberg, one of the great masters of wood engraving, renowned for the illustrations he created for literary classics, such as the novels of Dostoevsky and the Brontë sisters. Dorothy asked him if he would consider contributing some illustrations for *The Catholic Worker.* Eichenberg, a German Jew, had escaped Hitler's Germany, and later, after immigrating to the United States, had become a Quaker. He was deeply moved by her invitation. The fact that she couldn't pay him for his work, he said, "made it all the

more attractive." The Catholic Worker reflected his own pacifist leanings and his effort to see "that which is of God in every person." Along with his iconic illustrations for the *Worker,* Eichenberg would also provide illustrations for Day's memoir, *The Long Loneliness.*[10]

The choice of images was evidently left to him. Strikingly, he chose for the cover a depiction of the Annunciation—a gospel mystery that is not actually mentioned in her book. In his piece, we see an already pregnant Mary, evidently asleep, while an angel, hovering overhead, is whispering into her ear. Meanwhile, in the background, a winding road is leading ahead to Mount Calvary, where three crosses are already waiting.

It is a sign of Eichenberg's artistic vision that he chose to link the crucial turning point in Day's memoir—her decision to respond with gratitude to the gift of her unexpected pregnancy—with Mary's consent to accept her role in a divine plan beyond her comprehension: "Behold the handmaid of the Lord. May it be done unto me according to Thy will."

The whole history of salvation is encompassed in Mary's surrender. And it is renewed and extended in every act of faith—no matter how great or small. As Dag Hammarskjöld, the Swedish diplomat and mystic, wrote, "I don't know Who—or what—put the question. I don't know when it was put. I don't even remember answering. But at some moment I did answer Yes to Someone—or Something—and from that hour I was certain that existence is meaningful and that, therefore, my life, in self-surrender, had a goal."[11]

In the case of figures like Dorothy Day, Thomas Merton, and so many others, their holiness did not lie in any particular action, but in the constant effort, over a lifetime, to answer Yes—to follow where God was leading them. Their capacity for love, for friendship, their talents, their determination to be honest to God and to themselves about their faults, their impatience, their capacity for self-delusion—all were part of a life-long process of ongoing conversion, of ongoing consent to the enormous question posed by Someone—or Something.

But even in the case of the "official" saints, whose holiness, in retrospect, seems to fit them like a tailored outfit, we can see how much they struggled to find their way—a model of discipleship appropriate to their own gifts, or that responded to the needs of their time. So many of the "great" saints were inventors or innovators in this manner: St. Francis, of course, with his radical poverty; St. Teresa, who was inspired after many years as a Carmelite nun to undertake a radical reform of her order; St. Vincent de Paul; St. Ignatius Loyola; St. Joan of Arc, who accepted death rather than disavow the angelic "voices" that guided her; St. Benedict, whose monastic Rule set the standard for Western monasticism; St. Therese of Lisieux with her "Little Way"; Blessed Charles de Foucauld, with the long journey, via the Trappists and Nazareth, that led to his hermitage in the desert.

Mother Teresa as a young woman

Of course, in the case of such great, canonized saints, we tend to regard them as "finished products," their memory crowned with honor. But before Francis of Assisi was St. Francis, he was just Francesco di Bernardone, the son of a wealthy cloth merchant. Before he became St. Ignatius, Iñigo Lopez de Loyola was a vain young soldier. There was a time when the woman who became Mother Teresa was simply Sister Agnes, an Albanian nun working in her order's school in India. All of them started somewhere, in some unremarkable way, before venturing off the charts, taking a step into the unknown.

No matter where our vocation lies, God is always calling us to go deeper. Mistakes and false steps are part of the process, not simply a deviation. As the pope says, "In this quest to seek and find God in all things there is still an area of uncertainty. There must be. If a person says that he met God with total certainty and is not touched by a margin of uncertainty, then this is not good...If one has the answers to all the questions—that is the proof that God is not with him."[12]

In this process, conversion is not a once-and-for-all election of faith. In most cases, it is really a choice that must be constantly renewed or recalibrated in the course of an ongoing journey—a process of growing constantly in our capacity to love through the exercise of mercy, compassion, and forgiveness. As Thomas Merton wrote: "We are not 'converted' only once in our life but many times, and this endless series of large and small 'conversions,' inner revolutions, leads finally to our transformation in Christ."[13]

Looking back over my life it is possible to construct a narrative arc in which my encounters (whether in person or through books) with figures like St. Francis, Dorothy Day, Thomas Merton, Henri Nouwen, Flannery O'Connor, and Charles de Foucauld played central roles, drawing a straight line from my early youth right up to the present moment. But at any particular moment it didn't seem that way. Often the true significance of events in our lives becomes clear only when we look back and see the path they illuminated. We go one step at a time, and occasionally those steps involve some dramatic gestures, such as when St. Francis kissed a leper. But, as Dorothy Day said, "Sometimes it takes [just] one step. We would like to think so. And yet the older I get, the more I see that life is made up of many steps, and they are very small affairs, not giant strides. I have 'kissed a leper' not once, but twice—consciously—and I can't say I am any the better for it."[14]

Sometimes the providential twists and turns in my life have brought to mind the image of Tarzan, swinging from one vine to another, the next one seemingly always at hand when he needed it. And that instills a sense of trust and hope in what will come.

But that is only one side of the story. I could tell the story from a different perspective—the frequent times when my path was marked only by confusion and desolation, when all I could do was stretch out my empty hand, and the only prayer I could utter was "Help." Frederick Buechner, writing of the presence of God in our lives, says, "This does not mean that [God] makes events happen to us which move us in certain directions like chessmen. Instead, events happen under their own steam as random as rain, which means that God is present in them not as their cause but as the one who even in the hardest and most hair-raising of them offers us the possibility of that new life and healing which I believe is what salvation is."[15]

When I look back on my life and wonder, where was God in this story? I can easily see the great encounters, the opportunities, the doors that seemed to open just when I most needed them. But I have no doubt, as I look back, that God was also present in the times of failure, brokenness, and doubt. Perhaps the journey of faith is about learning to trust in "the possibility of new life and healing" even in the times when all seems dark and uncertain.

Father Steve DeMott

I WAS BLESSED TO WORK for some time with a holy Maryknoll priest, Fr. Steve DeMott, who served for many years among the poor in Chile. He was a man who embodied the Beatitudes— especially the spirit of poverty, the practice of mercy, and the challenge of peace. At the age of fifty he was diagnosed with an inoperable brain tumor. I found myself sitting next to him at a commemoration of the Maryknoll Sisters who had died in El Salvador. We were asked to turn to our neighbor and reflect on how we would live if we knew we might die the next day. Steve remarked: "Welcome to my world!"

We talked a lot about dying. I said I imagined he didn't have a lot of regrets. Oh, he said, he had a lot of regrets. He thought sometimes that he had been given an art project to complete. And he had gone about it in an indifferent way, working a bit here, a bit there, with a lot of distractions. And suddenly a voice was saying "Time's up!" And he felt such regret. But then he imagined Jesus saying to him, "You know, Steve, it wasn't really about the art project."

We often measure our lives by what we have accomplished, the monuments we have built, the legacy we will leave behind. But in the end it is good to be reminded that it is not really about the "art project," but about knowing and loving God and loving one another, in the short time that is given to us in this life. And perhaps our progress on this journey is marked not by our skill in identifying and grasping the next "vine," but in learning to let go, as Henri Nouwen put it, and trust in "the Catcher."

Our lives are not written out for us like an opera libretto, the pope says. We travel without any certainty of what lies ahead; sometimes we travel with the sun on our backs and sometimes in darkness. Sometimes we seem to lose our way. But we do not travel alone.

I have spent a large portion of my life reflecting on the saints, drawn not just by their heroic virtue and noble achievements but by the story that God tells us through their lives. By reading those stories, we may become more adept at discerning the presence of God in our own story.

Many years ago I happened to watch a Disney movie called *The Other Side of Heaven*, which tells the story of a young Mormon missionary in the South Pacific. After many trials and adventures he writes to his fiancée back home and sums up the lessons he has learned: "There is a thread that connects heaven and earth," he says. "If we find that thread everything is meaningful, even death. If we don't find it, nothing is meaningful, even life."

Sometimes I feel I have found that thread, only to lose it the very next moment. It is a thread that runs through the lives of Dorothy Day, Thomas Merton, and many of the saints, as it does through each of our lives—whether we acknowledge it or not. It is reminding us to be more loving, more truthful, more faithful in facing what Pope Francis in his "creed" calls "the surprise of each day."

To the extent that we respond to that reminder, as Jean-Pierre de Caussade wrote, "Our lives become a parchment; our sufferings and our actions are the ink. The workings of the Holy Spirit are the pen, and with it God writes a living gospel."[16]

ACKNOWLEDGMENTS

I AM DELIGHTED to publish this work with Orbis Books, which has been my working home for over half my life. My colleagues include Bernadette Price and Bill Medeot (with whom I have shared the entirety of these thirty-two years), Maria Angelini (who initially encouraged this project), Michael Lawrence, Jill O'Brien, Diana McDermott, Linda Mulvaney, Nancy Keels, and Doris Goodnough. I have been blessed to work with such friends and companions. In addition I am grateful to Celine Allen, both for her expert copyediting and her generous spirit, and to Roberta Savage for her cover design.

My thanks extend to the Maryknoll Fathers and Brothers, who launched this publishing house nearly fifty years ago and have supported it through years of feast, and more often famine. It has been a privilege to publish the work of brilliant, prophetic, and in many cases holy authors. Not by chance, they include the figures discussed in this book: Thomas Merton, Henri Nouwen, Charles de Foucauld, Flannery O'Connor, and of course Dorothy Day, who long ago planted the seeds of my eventual vocation.

Most of the chapters in this book had their origins in talks, retreats, and articles. I am grateful for the invitations that allowed me to test and elaborate these ideas at the Oblate School of Theology (San Antonio, TX), Yale Divinity School, St. Joseph College (Brooklyn, NY), Duquesne University (Pittsburgh, PA), Villanova University, the Maryknoll Mission Institute, and the Quidenham Carmelite Monastery in England. Some of the material also draws on my work in previous books, particularly *Blessed Among All Women, All Saints, The Saints' Guide to Happiness, The Franciscan Saints*, and *Blessed Among Us*. I am grateful to all the publishers of these works: Crossroad Publishing, Farrar Straus & Giroux, Image Books, Franciscan Media, and especially to Liturgical Press for inviting me to contribute daily reflections on saints for *Give Us This Day*.

Many friends have supported and encouraged my writing on saints over the years. I especially wish to thank Fr. John Dear, Sister Helen Prejean, Fr. William Hart McNichols, Sr. Elizabeth Johnson, Fr. Ron Rolheiser, Fr. James Martin, Alicia von Stamwitz, Peter Dwyer, Mary Stommes, Jim Forest, and Rachelle Linner.

Among the saints I have been blessed to know was Sister Wendy Beckett, who died on the day after Christmas, just as I was writing these last words. A contemplative hermit who lived on the grounds of the Carmelite Monastery in Quidenham, England, she became famous for her marvelous television programs on art for the BBC. But that was really a sideline from her true vocation of prayer. Somehow, in her last years, I drifted into her field of vision, and a spark occurred. It was as if the spirit of my mother had crossed with Julian of Norwich! In scores of sometimes daily letters, she responded with infinite wisdom, wit, and grace to my everyday thoughts, questions, and concerns. No topic was too insignificant for her attention or her blessing. She encouraged me to "believe in my life story" and to take seriously the work of "saint-watching." In one of her last letters, she commented on two of the figures treated in this book, Thomas Merton and Henri Nouwen: "There is

With Sr. Wendy Beckett

160

much self-deception and muddle in their lives, and yet there is an unwavering concentration on God. I think many people would find this very encouraging—that it's the direction that matters, the desire, and not the spiritual achievements, as it were." Someday, perhaps in a future book, I hope to do justice to her desire as well as her great achievements. In the meantime I am glad I could tell her that she would share the dedication of this book. I rejoice in her memory and I will try to honor her loving admonition "not to work too hard."

And finally, my deepest thanks to Monica, "a tender hawk," as Sister Wendy called her, an ongoing source of amazing grace.

NOTES

Introduction

1. Thomas Merton, *Life and Holiness* (New York: Image Books, 1964), 22–23.

2. See "Letter to 'A,'" December 16, 1955, *Flannery O'Connor: Spiritual Writings,* ed. Robert Ellsberg (Maryknoll, NY: Orbis Books, 2003), 76.

3. Merton, *Life and Holiness,* 24.

4. *Dorothy Day: Selected Writings,* ed. Robert Ellsberg (Maryknoll, NY: Orbis Books, 1992), 216.

5. Dorothy Day, *Therese* (Springfield, IL: 1960; reprint, Notre Dame, IN: Ave Maria, 2016), vii.

6. *All Saints: Daily Reflections on Saints, Prophets, and Witnesses for Our Time* (New York: Crossroad, 1997).

7. Simone Weil, *Waiting for God* (New York: Harper, 2009), 51.

8. Abraham Joshua Heschel, "No Religion Is an Island," in *No Religion Is an Island: Abraham Joshua Heschel and Interreligious Dialogue,* ed. Harold Kasimow and Byron L. Sherwin (Maryknoll, NY: Orbis Books, 1991), 18–19.

9. Robert Ellsberg, *Blessed Among Us: Day by Day with Saintly Witnesses* (Collegeville, MN: Liturgical Press, 2016).

10. Jean-Pierre de Caussade, *Abandonment to Divine Providence,* trans. John Beevers (New York: Image, 1993), 45.

11. St. Augustine, *Confessions,* trans. R. S. Pine-Coffin (New York: Penguin, 1961), 169.

12. Thomas Merton, *Search for Solitude: Pursuing the Monk's True Life, vol. 3, The Journals of Thomas Merton, 1953–1960,* ed. Lawrence S. Cunningham (New York: HarperOne, 1997), 359.

Chapter 1: The Call to Holiness

1. Pope Francis, *Rejoice and Be Glad: The Call to Holiness in Today's World* (Maryknoll, NY: Orbis Books, 2018).

2. See the pope's conversation with Antonio Spadaro, SJ, "A Big Heart Open to God," in *America* (September 30, 2013).

3. Reflections on St. Therese, Madeleine Delbrêl, and Daria Donnelly are adapted from Robert Ellsberg, *Blessed Among All Women* (New York: Crossroad, 2007).

4. Dorothy Day, *Therese* (Notre Dame, IN: Ave Maria, 2016), xv. See also my foreword to this edition.

5. Dorothy Day, *Loaves and Fishes* (Maryknoll, NY: Orbis Books, 2003), 176.

6. Delbrêl's writings, cited here, are included in Robert Ellsberg, ed., *Modern Spiritual Masters* (Maryknoll, NY: 2008), 53.

7. Ibid., 57.

8. Robert Ellsberg, *The Saints' Guide to Happiness* (New York: Image Books, 2005), 190.

Chapter 2: Reading God's Story

1. In Pope Francis, *I Believe: The Promise of the Creed*, ed. Stefan v. Kempis (Maryknoll, NY: Orbis Books, 2016), 2–3.

2. See Robert Ellsberg, *The Franciscan Saints* (Cincinnati: Franciscan Media, 2017).

3. The story of St. Alban appears in Bede's *History of the English Church and Its People*, written in the eighth century.

4. See *The Autobiography of St. Ignatius Loyola with Related Documents*, ed. John Olin (New York: Harper & Row, 1974).

5. Dorothy Day, *From Union Square to Rome* (Maryknoll, NY: Orbis Books, 2006), 26.

6. Ibid., 51.

7. Ibid., 91.

8. See *All the Way to Heaven: Selected Letters of Dorothy Day*, ed. Robert Ellsberg (New York: Image, 2012), 510, where she refers to these incidents.

9. St. Augustine, *The Confessions*, trans. R. S. Pine-Coffin (New York: Penguin, 1968), 72.

10. Dorothy Day, *The Long Loneliness* (New York: Harper & Row, 1952; HarperOne, 2009), 115.

11. Ibid., 148.

12. Ibid., 140.

13. Simone Weil, "Forms of the Implicit Love of God," in *Waiting for God* (New York: HarperCollins, 2001), 83–142.

14. Day, *From Union Square to Rome*, 11.

15. See Daniel Ellsberg, *Secrets: A Memoir of Vietnam and the Pentagon Papers* (New York: Viking, 2002).

16. *Dorothy Day: Selected Writings*, ed. Robert Ellsberg (Maryknoll, NY: Orbis Books, 1992), 354.

Chapter 3: Dorothy Day

1. *Dorothy Day: Selected Writings*, ed. Robert Ellsberg (Maryknoll, NY: Orbis Books, 1992), 51.

2. Visit to the Joint Session of the United States Congress, Address of the Holy Father, September 24, 2015. See w2.vatican.va.

3. Robert Ellsberg, "An Unusual History from the FBI," *Catholic Worker* (June 1979).

4. *Dorothy Day: Selected Writings*, 149.

5. Dorothy Day, *From Union Square to Rome* (Maryknoll, NY: Orbis Books, 2006), 19.

6. Dorothy Day, *The Long Loneliness* (HarperSanFrancisco, 1980), 116.

7. Ibid. 139.

8. Ibid., 136.

9. Day, *From Union Square to Rome*, 50.

10. Day, *The Long Loneliness*, 151.

11. Peter Maurin, "The Case for Utopia," *Easy Essays* (Chicago: Franciscan Herald Press, 1977), 37.

12. Maurin, "When Christ is King," *Easy Essays*, 61.

13. *Dorothy Day: Selected Writings*, 261–63.

14. Quoted in Jim Forest, *All Is Grace: A Biography of Dorothy Day* (Maryknoll, NY: Orbis Books, 2011), 337. See also Kate Hennessy, *Dorothy Day: The World Will Be Saved by Beauty* (New York: Scribners, 2017).

15. Dwight Macdonald, *Politics Past* (New York: Viking, 1970), 349.

16. Dorothy Day, "Letter to Jack English," December 31, 1953, *All the Way to Heaven: Selected Letters of Dorothy Day*, ed. Robert Ellsberg (Milwaukee: Marquette University Press, 2010), 218.

17. Dorothy Day, "Letter to Forster Batterham," September 21, 1925, *All the Way to Heaven: Selected Letters of Dorothy Day*, ed. Robert Ellsberg (Milwaukee: Marquette University Press, 2010), 12.

18. Day, "Letter to Forster Batterham," September 1925, *All the Way to Heaven*, 14.

19. Day, "Letter to Forster Batterham," September 16, 1929, *All the Way to Heaven*, 28.

20. Day, "Letter to Forster Batterham," December 10, 1932, *All the Way to Heaven*, 48.

21. Ibid.

22. Day, "Letter to Jim Forest," March 3, 1967, *All the Way to Heaven*, 332.

23. *The Duty of Delight: The Diaries of Dorothy Day*, ed. Robert Ellsberg (Milwaukee: Marquette University Press, 2008), 27.

24. Ibid., 60.

25. Ibid, 174.

26. Day, "Letter to Jack English," November 28, 1956, *All the Way to Heaven*, 239.

27. Day, "Letter to A Young Woman in Distress," February 6, 1973, *All the Way to Heaven*, 397.

28. Day, *The Duty of Delight*, 310.

29. Ibid., 509.

Chapter 4: Thomas Merton

1. Thomas Merton, *The Other Side of the Mountain. The Journals of Thomas Merton*, vol. 7: *1967–1968*, ed. Patrick Hart, OCSO (San Francisco: HarperSanFrancisco, 1998), 205.

2. Thomas Merton, *The Seven Storey Mountain* (New York: Harcourt, Brace, Jovanovich, 1948), 422–23.

3. Ibid.,181.

4. Ibid., 208.

5. Ibid., 237–38.

6. Ibid., 382.

7. Thomas Merton, *Secular Journal* (New York: Noonday Press, 1977), 183.

8. Merton, *Seven Storey Mountain,* 410.

9. Thomas Merton, *The Sign of Jonas* (New York: Image Books, 1956), 119.

10. Thomas Merton, *Conjectures of a Guilty Bystander* (New York: Image Books, 1968), 155.

11. Thomas Merton, *Solitude: Pursuing the Monk's True Life. The Journals of Thomas Merton, vol. 3: 1952–1960*, ed. Lawrence S. Cunningham (New York: HarperOne, 1997), 237.

12. Thomas Merton, *New Seeds of Contemplation* (New York: New Directions, 2007), 30.

13. Thomas Merton, *The Hidden Ground of Love: The Letters of Thomas Merton on Religious Experience and Social Concerns*, ed. William H. Shannon (New York: Harcourt, Brace, Jovanovich, 1993), 140.

14. Thomas Merton, "The Root of War Is Fear," in, *Passion for Peace: Reflections on War and Nonviolence*, ed. William H. Shannon (New York: Crossroad, 2006), 26.

15. Merton, *Conjectures of a Guilty Bystander*, 155.

16. Thomas Merton, *Contemplation in a World of Action* (New York: Image Book, 1973), 160.

17. Merton, *The Sign of Jonas*, 318.

18. Thomas Merton, *Introductions East and West: The Foreign Prefaces of Thomas Merton*, ed. Robert Daggy (Greensboro, NC: Unicorn Press, 1981), 45–46.

19. Merton, *Search for Solitude*, 285.

20. Ibid., 290.

21. Ibid., 236.

22. Ibid., 259.

23. Thomas Merton, *Turning toward the World: The Pivotal Years. The Journals of Thomas Merton, vol. 4: 1960–1963*, ed. Victor A. Kramer (New York: HarperOne, 1997), 79–80.

24. Thomas Merton, "A Signed Confessions of Crimes against the State," in *A Thomas Merton Reader*, ed. Thomas P. McDonnel (New York: Image Books, 1989), 117.

25. Thomas Merton, *The Wisdom of the Desert* (New York: New Directions, 1970), 5–6.

26. Thomas Merton, *Learning to Love: Exploring Solitude and Freedom. The Journals of Thomas Merton, vol. 6: 1966–1967*, ed. Christine M. Bochen (New York: HarperOne, 1998), 332.

27. Ibid., 162.

28. Ibid., 330.

29. *The Asian Journals of Thomas Merton*, ed. Patrick Hart, OCSO, et al. (New York: New Directions, 1975), 308.

30. Merton, *The Other Side of the Mountain*, 323.

31. *The Asian Journals*, 337.

32. Merton, *The Sign of Jonas*, 349.

33. Merton, *The Seven Storey Mountain*, 442.

34. Thomas Merton, *Dancing in the Waters of Life: Seeking Peace in the Hermitage. The Journals of Thomas Merton, vol. 5: 1963–1965*, ed. Robert E. Daggy (San Francisco: HarperSanFrancisco, 1997), 75.

35. Merton, *New Seeds of Contemplation*, 103.

36. Visit to the Joint Session of the United States Congress, Address of the Holy Father, September 24, 2015. See w2.vatican.va.

37. Pope Francis, *A Big Heart Open to God*, an interview with Antonio Spadaro, SJ (New York: HarperOne, 2013), 49.

Chapter 5: Henri Nouwen

1. Story recounted by Fred Bratman in *Befriending Life: Encounters with Henri Nouwen*, ed. Beth Porter (New York: Doubleday, 2001), 247.

2. Henri J. M. Nouwen, *The Genesee Diary: Report from a Trappist Abbey* (New York: Image Books, 1981), 13.

3. Ibid., 217.

4. See Henri J. M. Nouwen, *In the Name of Jesus: Reflections on Christian Leadership* (New York: Crossroad, 1993).

5. Henri J. M. Nouwen, *The Road to Daybreak: A Spiritual Journey* (New York: Image Books, 1990), 4.

6. Ibid., 81.

7. Ibid., 127.

8. Henri J. M. Nouwen, *The Inner Voice of Love: A Journey through Anguish to Freedom* (New York: Image Books, 1999), xiii.

9. Ibid., 118.

10. Henri J. M. Nouwen, *Sabbatical Journey: The Diary of His Final Year* (New York: Crossroad, 2000), 3.

11. Ibid., 61.

12. Henri J. M. Nouwen, *Our Greatest Gift: A Meditation on Dying and Caring* (New York: HarperOne, 2009), xvi.

13. Henri J. M. Nouwen, *Beyond the Mirror: Reflections on Life and Death* (New York: Crossroad, 2001), 47.

14. Ibid., 48.

15. Ibid., 78.

16. Nouwen, *Our Greatest Gift*, 63.

17. Ibid., 64.

18. Henri J. M. Nouwen, *Adam: God's Beloved* (Maryknoll, NY: Orbis Books, 1997), 36–37.

19. Ibid., 37.

20. Ibid., 127.

21. Ibid., 102.

22. Nouwen, *The Inner Voice of Love*, 118.

23. Nouwen, *Adam: God's Beloved*, 120.

24. Nouwen, *Sabbatical Journey*, 24.

Chapter 6: Flannery O'Connor

1. All the quotations cited in this essay are taken from *Flannery O'-Connor: Spiritual Writings*, ed. Robert Ellsberg (Maryknoll, NY: Orbis Books, 2003). References are to original sources. Letter to "A," July 5, 1958, *The Habit of Being: Letters of Flannery O'Connor*, selected and

edited by Sally Fitzgerald (New York: Farrar, Straus & Giroux, 1979), 290. Henceforth, *HB*.

2. Letter to "A," August 2, 1955, *HB*, 92.

3. Flannery O'Connor, "The Church and the Fiction Writer," in *Mystery and Manners: Occasional Prose,* ed. Sally and Robert Fitzgerald (New York: Farrar, Straus & Giroux, 1962), 146. Henceforth *MM*.

4. "Catholic Novelists and Their Readers," in *MM*, 173.

5. Letter to "A," August 2, 1955, *HB*, 92.

6. Letter to "A," September 6, 1955, *HB,* 100.

7. Ibid.

8. Letter to "A," August 2, 1955, *HB*, 92.

9. "The Fiction Writer & His Country," in *MM*, 34.

10. Letter to John Hawkes, September 13, 1959, *HB*, 349.

11. Author's note to 1962 edition of *Wise Blood* (New York: Farrar, Straus & Giroux, 1962). Included in *Three by Flannery O'Connor* (New York: Signet Book, n.d.), 8. Henceforth, *WB*.

12. *WB*, 24.

13. Ibid., 16.

14. Ibid., 60.

15. Ibid.

16. Ibid., 116, 118, 119.

17. Ibid., 119.

18. Ibid., 126.

19. Letter to Elizabeth and Robert Lowell, March 17, 1953. *HB, 57.*

20. Pierre Teilhard de Chardin discusses his idea of "passive diminishment" in *The Divine Milieu* (New York: Harper & Row, 1965), 74–93.

21. From O'Connor's "Introduction to *A Memoir of Mary Ann,*" in *MM*, 223.

22. "A Good Man is Hard to Find," *Flannery O'Connor: The Complete Stories* (New York: Farrar, Straus & Giroux, 1971), 133.

23. See "Introduction to *A Memoir of Mary Ann,*" in *MM*.

24. Letter to John Lynch, November 6, 1955, *HB*, 114.

25. Letter to "A," July 20, 1955, *HB*, 90.

26. Ibid.

27. Richard Giannone, "Flannery O'Connor's Dialogue with the Age," Introduction to *Flannery O'Connor: Spiritual Writings,* ed. Robert Ellsberg (Maryknoll, NY: Orbis Books, 2003), 31.

28. Letter to Dr. T. R. Spivey, June 21, 1959, *HB*, 337.

29. "Catholic Novelists and Their Readers," in *MM, 78.*

30. See Letter to Roslyn Barnes, December 12, 1960, *HB,* 422.

31. Letter to Alfred Corn, May 30, 196, *HB*, 476-78.

32. Letter to "A," June 28, 1956, *HB*, 163.

33. Letter to "A," February 4, 1961, *HB*, 430.

34. Ibid.

35. "Prayer to Saint Raphael," *HB*, 592–93.

Chapter 7: Charles de Foucauld

1. The sources for this essay include: Charles Hillyer, *Charles de Foucauld* (Collegeville, MN: Liturgical Press, 1990); Charles Lepetit, *Two Dancers in the Desert: The Life of Charles de Foucauld* (Tunbridge Wells: Burns & Oates, and Maryknoll, NY: Orbis Books, 1983); *A Little Brother of Jesus, Silent Pilgrimage to God: The Spirituality of Charles de Foucauld* (London: Darton, Longman and Todd, and Maryknoll, NY: Orbis Books, 1974); Marion Mill Preminger, *The Sands of Tamanrasset* (New York: Hawthorn Books, 1961); *Spiritual Autobiography of Charles de Foucauld*, ed. Jean-François Six (New York: P. J. Kenedy & Sons, 1964); Jean-François Six, *Witness in the Desert: The Life of Charles de Foucauld* (New York: Macmillan, 1965); Margaret Trouncer, *Charles de Foucauld* (London: George G. Harrap, 1972).

Chapter 8: Holy Women

1. Dorothy Day, *From Union Square to Rome* (Maryknoll, NY: Orbis Books, 2006), 61.

2. Mark Danner, "The Truth of El Mozote," *The New Yorker* (December 6, 1993): 50ff.

3. See Mary Oliver, IBVM, *Mary Ward* (New York: Sheed & Ward, 1959).

4. See *Hildegard of Bingen: Mystical Writings*, ed. Fiona Bowie and Oliver Davis (New York: Crossroad, 1995).

5. See Penny Blaker Mitchell, *Mother Theodore Guerin: A Woman for Our Time* (St. Mary-of-the-Woods, IN: Office of Congregational Advancement, Sisters of Providence, 1998).

6. See Annemarie Sanders, IHM, *However Long the Night: Making Meaning in a Time of Crisis: A Spiritual Journey of the Leadership Conference of Women Religious* (Scotts Valley, CA: Createspace, 2018).

7. See Penny Lernoux, with Arthur Jones and Robert Ellsberg, *Hearts on Fire: The Story of the Maryknoll Sisters* (Maryknoll, NY: Orbis Books, 1993, 2011); Claudette LaVerdiere, MM, *On the Threshold of the Future: The Life and Spirituality of Mother Mary Joseph Rogers, Founder of the Maryknoll Sisters* (Maryknoll, NY: Orbis Books, 2011).

Chapter 9: A Journey Faith

1. Antonio Spadaro, SJ, "A Big Heart Open to God: An interview with Pope Francis," *America,* September 30, 2013. Also published in book form, with commentary, *A Big Heart Open to God: A Conversation with Pope Francis* (New York: HarperOne, 2013).

2. Ibid., 59.

3. Ibid., 60.

4. Ibid., 14.

5. Ibid., 16.

6. Ibid., 49.

7. Gordon Zahn, *In Solitary Witness: The Life and Death of Franz Jägerstatter* (Springfield, IL: Templegate, rev. ed. 1986). See also *Franz Jägerstatter: Letters and Writings from Prison*, ed. Erna Putz (Maryknoll, NY: Orbis Books, 2009).

8. Thomas Merton, *Thoughts in Solitude* (New York: Farrar Straus & Giroux, 1999), 79.

9. Henri J. M. Nouwen, *Sabbatical Journey: The Diary of His Final Year* (New York: Crossroad, 2000), 133.

10. See *Fritz Eichenberg: Works of Mercy*, ed. Robert Ellsberg (Maryknoll, NY: Orbis Books, 1992).

11. Dag Hammarskjöld, *Markings* (New York: Vintage, 2006), 133.

12. *A Big Heart*, 48.

13. Thomas Merton, *Life and Holiness* (New York: Image, 1964), 117.

14. *Dorothy Day: Selected Writings*, ed. Robert Ellsberg (Maryknoll, NY: Orbis Books, 1992), 110.

15. Frederick Buechner, *Telling Secrets* (New York: HarperOne, 2000), 31.

16. Jean-Pierre de Caussade, *Abandonment to Divine Providence* (New York: Image, 1993), 45.

INDEX